A CALL TO ACTION

HOW TO SAVE MILLIONS OF LIVES

ERIC KAUFMAN
JOAQUIN F. MATIAS, Co-Author / Editor

KLAUS JACOB, Introduction
Donovan Burton, Foreword

ISBN-13: 978-069282970

Printed through www.createspace.com /
Amazon All rights reserved

General interior design by Joaquin F. Matias
Publication design and layout by Ava Fedorov
Cover design by Ava Fedorov

"Never doubt that a small group of
concerned citizens can change the world.
Indeed, it is the only thing that ever has."

Margaret Mead

DEDICATED TO
OUR MILLENNIALS AND
POST MILLENNIALS

Proceeds from this book to be donated to
The Natural Resilience Fund, Inc. (d/b/a
The Natural Resilience Foundation), 501(c)3

CONTENTS

FOREWORD

What a time to write a foreword for what I believe is a timely and considered book. I have just arrived back from the latest international climate change negotiations at Marrakesh (COP22) in time to witness the birth of my first son, the new driver for my work in resilience planning. So much needs to be done to ensure that we create an economy that both reduces global greenhouse gas emissions and responds to those effects of climate change that are already locked into the system. While the implementation of action is challenging, the response momentum has reached the tipping point. And this tipping point is occurring at the peak of a technological renaissance which is facilitating innovation, disruption and collaboration in facing what looks, to some, like an insurmountable challenge.

New technologies present an endless abundance of opportunities. For example, I met Eric Kaufman during one of my late-night LinkedIn stalking sessions – an activity that was unheard-of ten years ago, but now fosters a network of global knowledge. My online engagement with Eric soon transposed into a real-life meeting in New York's Central Park with him at his home (where I also met his business partner, Joaquin), from where our professional relationship blossomed into a true friendship and collaboration on resilience development. While in the US I was fortunate enough to see some of that great technological innovation (and collaboration) when I attended VERGE 2015 in Silicon Valley – a conference where sustainability blends with the Internet of Things. The collaborative economy is emerging rapidly. There is a genuine buzz and openness for shared solutions.

Recently many of my colleagues in the US have expressed deep concern about the potential challenges in US climate policy.

Rightly so. However, I can already see Eric's "solution radar" kicking in – making this book all that timelier. This book is a call to action, which presents both the stark challenges that we face together with realistic responses, based on a combination of working case studies and visionary thinking. I originally trained as an urban and environmental planner and the foresight displayed by Eric and Joaquin reminds me of some of the visionary planners who helped shape human settlement patterns and deal with the environmental challenges during the onset of the Industrial Revolution.

A Call to Action: How to Save Millions of Lives is an important read. I hope that this book inspires people to respond to the effects of climate change. There is a place for all responses: from civil disobedience to market forces and innovative technologies. The insights Eric and Joaquin provide here will pay valuable dividends to investors, property developers and politicians in creating a wealth of opportunities while preparing for our common future.

Donovan Burton
Climate Planning

Donovan Burton is the founder of Climate Planning, an international climate change adaptation consultancy. Having completed over 130 climate change adaptation projects in the past decade he is widely recognized as a leader in his field. Donovan has worked with UN agencies, insurers, property developers, infrastructure providers, area research organizations and all levels of government providing a range of climate change adaptation services. Donovan is a systems specialist who focuses in climate change adaptation governance and identifying emerging opportunities associated with adaptation. His work has been presented at various UN conferences and the World Economic Forum in Davos.

Currently residing in Australia, Donovan has authored many publications. He is a graduate of Griffith University in environmental planning (honors first class).

AUTHORS' LETTER

Some of the ideas put forth in this book may seem very foreign to people. The field of climate resilience is still emerging, but we will have no choice but to live with the impact of a changing weather environment. Only by understanding its far-reaching consequences can we learn how to better prepare ourselves for it.

This book is motivated by a reality almost certain to occur between now and 2050, in which a number of climate shocks will force the planet and all forms of life, including us humans and animals, to adapt to changing weather conditions. James Lovelock explains in his thought-provoking *Gaia* series of writings that earth (Gaia) is a living organism that will adapt to changing weather conditions to suit her long-term survival. What we should be concerned about is whether we, humans, as a species, can adapt as well.

I began and developed the general contours of this book, drawn from my intensive study of climate resilience during the last four years and my travels throughout the many places we mention from Colombia and The Netherlands to states within the U.S. such as West Virginia, Georgia, North Carolina and Texas. I share these and other personal experiences throughout. Joaquin joined me as a co-author as he developed many of the concepts utilized by the Natural Resilience Foundation.

Together, we will be exploring ideas, many of which are already implementable, to help address the challenges arising from changing weather patterns. Though it will be the Millennial and Post-Millennial Generations – a span of some five decades – who will be experiencing and living in these very changed circumstances; we (along with them) must begin that work now on behalf of their future. In the <u>Glossary</u> at the end of this book, we explain the terms we use and additional ones used in the fields of climate change, sustainability and economic and real estate development. We highlight these terms in green when they first appear and from time to time so you can see how many of these concepts are related. We hope in this way that science does not get in the way of our larger concept of preparing ourselves through relocation communities.

We hope to provide you with some insights, direction and guidance to ready ourselves for the effects of climate change, both to slow it down as well as develop contingency strategies such as establishing relocation cities and communities.

We also ask you to consider with us the constraints that our current economic, political, psychological and sociological viewpoints – that we call the EPPS Syndrome – will have in slowing down or even impeding the kind of large-scale action needed to save potentially millions of lives from the effects of climate change. Our inability to act now will only make it more difficult and costlier to our Millennials and Post Millennials. We may very well have to go beyond merely putting aside these current constraints by shifting these perspectives towards acting collectively, kindly and generously. The thought leaders, the precedents and the ideas we provide are intended to open this kind of conversation. In this way we believe the millions (and multi-millions) seeking refuge from climate devastation can have a true alternative.

Our call to action centers on the need to set up, as quickly as possible, sustainable and resilient relocation communities of all sizes, especially ones of larger scale. The establishment, build-ing and repurposing activities connected with starting these sus-tainable, resilient communities will be powerful catalysts for economic development, generate a significant number of jobs and open opportunities for utilizing technology and innovation – all of which shall strengthen those areas where these relocation communities and cities will be situated. These sustainable and resilient communities will be the alternative for residents who face the challenges of living, for example, in low-lying areas, by unprotected coasts, or in water-constrained and drought-stricken areas. Many will also benefit from employment opportunities and a sustainable way of life. At some point soon, we also envision the need to scale up the number of these relocation communities and cities within the U.S. and globally so they can absorb the millions who will be facing "forced" displacement by extreme weather.

Some, even many, people may want to remain in places they have called home – homes where they may have lived in for many generations. The choices they will face will be painful: between a life they've known in locations that may no longer be possible and a life of new possibilities in areas more resilient to extreme weather events. As the impact of extreme weather events increases in frequency and intensity and affects growing numbers of people, fewer and fewer municipalities will be able to justify the allocation of their limited resources to safeguard a single family, community or even an area over the needs of hundreds of thousands; even a million or so of its other residents.

Just as the earth itself will have to contend with the effects of weather change, massive numbers of people, too, will be forced to undertake The Great Climate Diaspora. This diaspora will be a migration from the south to the north, towards and into safer, climate resilient places such as the Scandinavian countries, the Northern United States, Canada and Siberia and, possibly even, Greenland.

A Call to Action urges us and our Millennials and Post-Millennials to think long-term and take concrete actions to plan, design, construct and move to sustainable and resilient self-contained communities.

Eric Kaufman
Joaquin F. Matias
The Natural Resilience Foundation

ACKNOWLEDGEMENTS

Back in 2013 when we formed the NRF, the old ways of doing business and the distinctions over being "for profit" or "not for profit" were giving way to collaboration as the new competitive model. We've drawn from a rich tapestry of individuals and organizations across the globe, reflecting nearly all age groups and political perspectives. We are proud to be among that new breed of companies where collaboration is key. We hope we do justice to those mentioned in these acknowledgements.

As the principal founder of The NRF, Eric makes this first set of acknowledgements to his partners (and board members) at The NRF. Joaquin F. Matias has contributed his wide-ranging talents and expertise in strategy, communications, public policy and economic development. He has benefited The NRF with his unique ability to take a concept, think it through and develop the policies, white papers and implementation plans. James-Robert Sellinger has provided us his grounded energy, willingness to listen, reflect and offer valuable insight and measured counsel. At the same time he is pushing the envelope in developing forward-thinking financing strategies to move us toward a non-fossil fuel-based economy.

Playing an important role in the evolution of The NRF, we thank Marty Katz for providing us with valuable marketing insight that led to our work with Built Environment. He generously expanded our circle of advisors and professional contacts. Steve Wilson helped us develop our international network and contributed to our view of climate change within the context of threat multipliers. Of special note, we also thank David Gibson for the time he took (along with Michael Sackler) to think through the relationship between sustainability and resiliency; his deep insight as an early adopter in sustainability was key.

On the level of thought leadership, we at The NRF are deeply indebted to Klaus Jacob, Senior Research Scientist, Seismology, Geology and Tectonophysics at the Lamont-Doherty Earth Observatory of Columbia University, for his concept of relocating people upland and out of flood zones as well as his concept of nomadic infrastructure. We greatly appreciated as well the time that Henk Ovink, Donovan Burton and Susannah Drake have each contributed to the development of our ideas and strategies. They are among the most innovative thinkers and practitioners in this field.

Over the years, we valued the feedback and insights provided by a network of professionals and experts including Cynthia Arnson, Diego Bermúdez, Lauren Burnhill, Victoria Cabanos, Frank DeLucia, Tom and Leslie Donovan, Janine Finnell, Donald Giampietro, Guy Gioino, Ann Goodman, Philip M. Hecht, Denise Katzman, Carmen and Juan Lacambra, Fernanda Leite, Peter Miller, Dominic Molloy, Gita Nandan and Meenakshi Varandani.

Our work has taken us beyond the realm of concepts and idealistic thinking as we have developed (and continue to develop) working partnerships with providers and manufacturers of sustainable energy-systems like cogen and trigen models being built by the Intelligen Power Systems with Sardil Anam, Sal Cona and David Lesser. We have especially enjoyed blue-skying and learning about geothermal systems and cutting-edge water management strategies from our friends in the Netherlands, particularly Gerwin Hop.

We thank Musa Asad, Richard Kusack and, again, Marty Katz for working on seed financing, potential partnerships and collaborations.

For the publishing of this book, we are grateful for the early advice given by Allie Benjamin; the fine photos shared by Arlen Stawasz who is both a talented architect and an expert photographer; Kelly Witter for her perspective and efforts to get the word out; and Jose Roberto Gutierrez for his marketing and communications acumen. As a special note, we thank Jon Scher for his thoughtful evaluation and strategic advice that draws from his expertise and insight as a journalist. Special, heartfelt thanks to Ava Fedorov for designing the book cover and getting us through the final stage of graphics, design and flow checks. Her patience saw us through the launching of this book on the publishing platform and working out the technical kinks.

Finally, Eric thanks his family – Joan Kaufman, Ellie Sugarman (also a board member of The NRF), Patti Kaufman, Parker Shannon (who also gave us his take on Plan Relocation), Cassie Forward, Alex Kaufman, Keara Forward and Ella Wiznia – for their long-standing support at The NRF. Joaquin thanks his parents, Amelia and Romy (an inveterate entrepreneur and businessman); his partner, Jon Scher; and great friend, Roberto Gutierrez. They have given generously in these endeavors.

We end with a message of thanks to YOU, the reader and the over 6,000 LinkedIn contacts for contributing in your way to the NRF and its efforts. Your support in the form of passing this book and its call to action to others as well as making a donation to support The NRF's continuing efforts are vital!

Eric Kaufman
Joaquin Matias
The Natural Resilience Foundation

INTRODUCTION

A Call to Action is a mind-boggling, kaleidoscopic tour-de-force ranging from the utopian to the very urgent and practical. It is all but an academic essay born from the conviction that anything less than transformative measures will not do to turn economic, political, psychological and sociological inertia into viable opportunities; or molding mere efforts to just survive the now inevitable threats from climate change, into economic and urban revival.

I am not an economist, but I read with fascination the various proposals to finance this call for transformation via such measures as tax credits and other financial instruments, all very far from my skills as an Earth scientist, who has been, expertly yet cluelessly, concerned for too long how we might adapt to the "new normal" of coastal cities being inundated and how land-bound cities might sustainably quench their thirst for potable water. Yes, **A Call to Action** pays its tribute to doom and gloom that, just relying on science-based climate forecasts, is well justified.

But what's striking in this treatise is the purveying and persuasive optimism, spiced with innovative ideas and practical proposals, to cope with the inevitabilities of climate change. **A Call to Action** is an amazing tour guide for how to avoid the unavoidable. It will take a generation of citizens, economists, politicians, business leaders and followers alike, and tons of investments, to translate this call into much needed action; and beyond, into truly sustainable human and urban resilience. **A Call to Action** is a visionary manifesto for how to secure a brighter future that, with collective will, may allow us to skirt the abyss of inaction.

Klaus H. Jacob
December 31, 2016

Dr. Jacob is a geophysicist with Columbia University since 1968. His most recent research since 2000 focuses on quantitative assessment of risks from climate change, sea-level rise and coastal storms for global megacities, with special focus on New York City and its infrastructure. He teaches graduate courses on Disaster Risk Management and Sustainable Urban Resilience at Columbia's School of Professional Studies, and did so earlier for a decade at its School of International and Public Affairs. Based at Columbia's Lamont-Doherty Earth Observatory, he carried out seismic research for more than 40 years. He also taught at Columbia's Graduate School of Architecture, Preservation and Planning, developing master plans for Caracas, Istanbul and Accra to improve resilience against earthquakes and other hazards. He helped cofound the National Center for Earthquake Engineering Research (NCEER), worked on seismic risk assessment projects in 5 continents; contributed to NYC's first seismic building code and the NEHRP national seismic model code. He performed modal analysis of large bridges and buildings in the Greater NYC Metro region. He is a member of the Seismological Society of America, the Earthquake Engineering Research Institute, and the American Geophysical Union. In 2008 Mayor Bloomberg appointed him to the New York City Panel on Climate Change (NPCC) on which he still serves today. Time Magazine named him one of globally 50 *People who Mattered in 2012*, for his detailed forecast of the likely impacts of a severe coastal storm on New York City, that was eerily validated by Superstorm Sandy only one year after the report's publication.

CHAPTER 1
Executive Summary

For the past four years, Eric has been studying climate resilience and how to protect the built environment against the effects of weather events. Much of what we hear have been debates over whether these climate changes result from man-made activity or not, or whether we can reverse what has been already set in motion. Still we face the reality of increasing frequency and severity of extreme weather events – a reality that over a relatively short period will force us to choose how and where we live. This soon-to-be reality will test our will to survive by living in a new way over remaining as we are with our homes being repeatedly destroyed and ravaged by extreme weather.

At The Natural Resilience Foundation (NRF), along with our colleagues and collaborators, we see that the best strategy for climate resilience is one that combines sustainability (mitigation) measures with resilience (adaptation) efforts. In Chapter 7, we examine how sustainability and resiliency together form an integrated solution as well as identify the other elements needed to implement this solution such as financing sources, public, private and community partnerships, and a decision-making process informed by experts. One of the financing strategies we explore is the S + R Paradigm, as we term it, in which the energy savings achieved through sustainable practices helps finance the cost of these massive and expensive infrastructure resiliency projects. At the same time, designing an integrated S + R system from the start would result in a stronger, more resilient solution.

Our embrace of the green economy follows from the millions of jobs that can be created while at least slowing down the increase of fossil fuel emissions. Lester R. Brown, founder of Worldwatch Institute/Earth Policy Institute, placed the green economy at the centerpiece of his Plan B to "save the civilization." In Chapter 5, as advocates of Plan B, we consider its various dimensions. Should we take a page out of the playbook used during the Great Depression of the 1930's, when the Works Progress Administration undertook vast public works, we could build green, sustainable and resilient infrastructure that will enable our Millennials and Post Millennials to survive and also prosper in the face of climate change.

In the COP 21 / Paris Agreement of December 2015, 195 countries agreed to reduce their carbon emissions in an amount sufficient to limit global warming to not more than 2° Celsius (about 3.6° Fahrenheit) and work towards a more aggressive goal of reducing warming to no more than 1.5° C (about 2.7° F). This is a first and necessary step in the right direction. In Chapter 8, we consider some of the technologies that might help us achieve these goals – as many solutions are already available to us. But it remains to be seen, particularly under the mantle of President Donald Trump of the United States, whether our country along with the other member signatories, who we see as representatives of our species, will have the public and political will to carry this out. For more details on this historic agreement, take time to review Appendix A.

At the same time, we believe we must develop a contingency plan should Brown's Plan B or the Paris Agreement not be undertaken quickly enough, or at a scale sufficient to stem CO_2 emissions. Our Plan Relocation (Plan R), which we introduce in Chapter 11 and explore in depth in Chapter 13, envisions the "relocation" of millions facing dislocation by extreme weather events into sustainable rural communities, large-scale urban developments and high-rise mega-cities. Throughout the book we will refer to these as relocation communities and cities, relocation sites or sustainable, resilient communities and cities.

Relocation to these sustainable communities and mega-cities are not unlike the migrations animal communities are undertaking because of changing weather patterns. Presaged by the animals searching for food and water today, we, humans, too, may be desperately searching for food, water and shelter in the relative near future.

Humans are projected to number 9 billion by 2050 – only 34 years from the date of this writing. Those of us living in less affected or even non-affected areas may find it difficult to understand the impact of changing weather events happening around the planet. But make no mistake these weather events are occurring in real time.

We offer up several cases to give you perspective on their challenges and experiences: the Netherlands and Bangladesh in Chapter 10, Cartagena, Colombia in Chapter 17, and those within the U.S. in Austin, Texas, and the coal-mining towns of West Virginia in Chapters 15 and 16. Throughout we also refer to the experiences in New Orleans, Louisiana; Princeville, North Carolina; Miami, Florida; Rockaways and Lower Manhattan, New York; and various areas in California.

Joaquin sees our efforts here as being about what we want for ourselves, for our children and for the human race in an environment that is changing. He envisions **A Call to Action** as a reframing around preparing ourselves and how we can create tremendous opportunities in how we live, how we define community and the kinds of jobs and quality housing we can create in this process. This reframing will interest emerging architects and urban planners as they wrestle with the issues of tomorrow; provide practical strategies for government officials seeking to revitalize their communities and cities; investors, insurance and energy companies exploring new investment opportunities as well as wanting to protect their current assets; and real estate developers and community builders who know well the process of renewal, rebuilding and regrowth.

This summary chapter ends with a cautionary note. Some of us may have thought ourselves as planet savers; but the fact is Mother Earth will be fine. She will adapt as she did by freezing over during the last ice age, or heating up and generating the level of volcanic activity that resulted in changed land formations. For our part, we need to focus on being species savers, with a particular focus on saving our own species.

View of newly constructed World Trade Center transit station designed by Santiago Calatrava. Source: Eric Kaufman (2016)

CHAPTER 2
Where Do We Go from Here?

Eric has been exploring how the newly emerging field of climate resilience along with sustainability will impact the built environment. Together both fields will be important in stemming the tide of global warming and its impact for our species and others. Being a part of something genuinely meaningful and being surrounded by similarly impassioned people has excited him and given him some basis for believing that people will realize that a "Green Revolution" is necessary for us.

And then, it dawned on Eric – the true nature of human beings is to procrastinate; react rather than plan; debate, argue, fight or hope for the best – all attempts to resist the daunting challenge of change. This admixture cloaked in the most dangerous of behaviors, hubris, does not bode well when collective and decisive action is needed to address the effects of rapidly changing weather events.

Elizabeth Kolbert in *The Sixth Extinction* (the Anthropocene epoch) provides a "wonderfully tactile sense of endangered (or already departed) species and their shrinking habitats"[1] as a result of man's "transformation of the ecological landscape."[2] Kolbert writes:

> It is estimated that one-third of all reef-building corals, a third of all freshwater mollusks, a third of sharks and rays, a quarter of all mammals, a fifth of all reptiles, and a sixth of all birds are headed toward oblivion. The losses are occurring all over: in the South Pacific and in the North Atlantic, in the Arctic and the Sahel, in lakes and on islands, on mountaintops and in valleys.

History can be difficult to verify but the consensus is that previous extinctions were not man-made. Reasons range from asteroids hitting our planet to rapid cooling of the planet's surface; these resulted in rapid climate change on earth. Viviene Richter in *Cosmos Magazine* defined these five mass extinctions[3] with the following taken from her article. Some very small changes in text have been made for greater clarity.

THE FIVE BIG EXTINCTIONS

> Biologists suspect we're living through the sixth major mass extinction. Earth has witnessed five, when more than 75% of species disappeared. Paleontologists spot them when species go missing from the global fossil record, including the iconic specimens shown here. "We don't always know what caused them but most had something to do with rapid climate change," says Melbourne Museum paleontologist Rolf Schmidt.

End of Ordovician 444 million years ago during which 86% of species was lost. Image of Graptolite 2-3 cm length. Credit: Jaime Murcia / Museum Victoria

1ˢᵗ Extinction. Graptolites, like most Ordovician life, were sea creatures. They were filter-feeding animals and colony builders. Their demise over about a million years was probably caused by a short, severe ice age that lowered sea levels, possibly triggered by the uplift of the Appalachians. The newly exposed silicate rock sucked CO_2 out of the atmosphere and chilled the planet.

End of Late Devonian 375 million years ago during which 75% of species was lost. Image of Trilobite, 5 cm length. Credit: Jaime Murcia / Museum Victoria

2ⁿᵈ Extinction. Trilobites were the most diverse and abundant of the animals that appeared in the Cambrian explosion 550 million years ago. With their spiky armor and multi-faceted eyes they survived the first great extinction. They were nearly wiped out in the second extinction likely because of the newly evolved land plants that emerged during the Devonian period and covered the planet. Their deep roots stirred up the earth, releasing nutrients into the ocean, and in turn possibly triggering algal blooms that sucked oxygen out of the water and suffocated bottom dwellers like the trilobites.

End of Permian 251 million years ago during which 96% of species was lost. Image of Tabulate coral, 5 CM. Credit: C. Clark / Smithsonian Institution

3ʳᵈ Extinction. Known as "the great dying," this was the worst extinction event ever seen. It nearly ended life on Earth such as the tabulate corals, which form today's corals. A perfect storm of natural catastrophes assailed the planet: a cataclysmic eruption near Siberia blasted CO_2 into the atmosphere; methanogenic bacteria responded by belching out methane, a potent greenhouse gas; a surge in global temperatures; and acidification and stagnation of the oceans that belched poisonous hydrogen sulfide. "It set life back 300 million years," says Schmidt. Rocks after this period record no coral reefs or coal deposits.

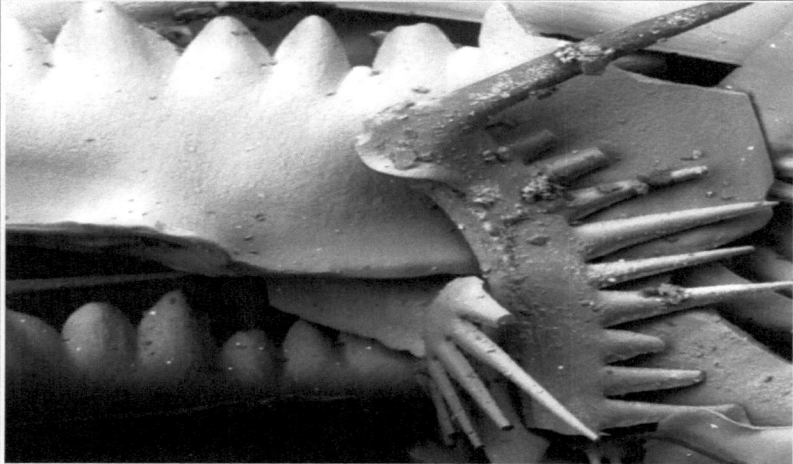

End of Triassic 200 million years ago during which 80% of species was lost. Image of Conodont teeth 1 mm. Credit: Natural History Museum, London

4ᵗʰ Extinction.

Paleontologists were baffled about the origin of these toothy fragments, mistaking them for bits of clams or sponges. The discovery of an intact fossil in Scotland in the 1980s finally revealed their owner – a jawless eel-like vertebrate named the conodont with this remarkable set of teeth lining its mouth and throat. They were one of the first structures built from hydroxyapatite, a calcium-rich mineral that remains a key component of our own bones and teeth today. Of all the great extinctions, the one that ended the Triassic is the most enigmatic. No clear cause has been found.

End of Cretaceous 66 million years ago during which 76% of all species was lost.
Image of Ammonite 15 cm length. Credit: Jaime Murcia / Museum Victoria

5ᵗʰ Extinction. The delicate, leaf-like sutures decorating this shell represent some advanced engineering, providing the fortification the squid-like ammonite required to withstand the pressure of deep dives when pursuing its prey. Dinosaurs may have ruled the land during the Cretaceous period but the oceans belonged to the ammonites. But volcanic activity and climate change placed the ammonites under stress with an asteroid impact, which ended the dinosaurs' reign, being the final blow. Only a few dwindling species of ammonites survived. Today, the ammonites' oldest surviving relative is the nautilus. Will it survive the next extinction?

The sixth extinction is called Anthropocene, the era of human beings. How will it end? Will our extinction result from flood, fire or drought? Most likely a mix of these events and, even possibly, an extraneous event like a collision with another planetary body will deal the lethal blow.

As human beings, we do not know the full ramifications of these and other planetary and cosmic influences; this is simply out of our pay grade.

REASONS FOR CLIMATE CHANGE

Most scientists observe that the earth is warming due primarily to fossil fuel emissions and human behavior. Debate continues whether such climate warming is man-made or not; or even if such global warming is occurring. For example, there has been some recent controversy that the "loss of glacier mass in Antarctica's western region is being offset by thickening of glaciers on the continent's eastern interior."[4]

What you will read here is that there is very strong evidence that global warming is occurring.

> A peer-review of all (over 12,000) peer-reviewed abstracts on the subject 'global climate change' and 'global warming' published between 1991 and 2011 (Cook et al. 2013) found that over 97% of the papers taking a position on the subject agreed with the consensus position that humans are causing global warming. In a second phase of the project, the scientist authors were emailed and rated over 2,000 of their own papers. Once again, over 97% of the papers taking a position on the cause of global warming agreed that humans are causing it.[5]

Theories about the causes of global warming include: thinning of the atmosphere, use of fossil fuels, waste, poor agricultural practices and others. The National Climate Assessment observes that human influences are the number one cause of global warming, especially as the burning of fossil fuels causes carbon pollution. Carbon dioxide (or CO_2), methane, soot and the other pollutants that we release into the atmosphere act like a blanket by trapping the sun's heat and warming the planet. Such an effect is similar to glass greenhouses constructed to keep plants inside much warmer than ambient cooler temperature by letting in and keeping in the sun's heat.

The level of carbon dioxide, even after being absorbed by forests and oceans, is still increasing by almost 3 parts per million (ppm) between 2014 and 2015 up to 399 ppm in 2015.[6] This and other data indicate CO_2 has been increasing annually on average by 1.76 ppm since 1979; with a much greater increase during the last five years of 2.5 ppm.[7] Methane, too, has been increasing. Its increase, measured in parts per billion (ppb), was 11 ppb from 2014 to 2015. This one-year increase almost doubled from 2007 – 2013.[8] A rise in methane is especially disturbing as it "traps heat 25 times more effectively than carbon dioxide. It accounts for about 10.6% of U.S. greenhouse gas emissions."[9]

Evidence shows that the period, 2000 to 2009, was hotter than any other decade during the past 1,300 years. This warming is altering in far-reaching ways the earth's climate system, including its land, atmosphere, oceans and ice. Such global warming is affecting and melting the polar ice caps, the ice sheets and glaciers, which in turn result in sea level rise. As this melting occurs, we can expect dramatic and significant sea level rise that will affect most especially coastal cities. In a contrasting, simultaneous way, global warming is, by increasing temperatures, causing long drought periods.

Cutting across the effects of too much water or too little water, we have a third result – subsidence – in which land is sinking from "cracks in the earth caused by prolonged dry spells"; from drawing groundwater from aquifers below; and from the rising seas along coastal "sinking" megacities that are built on thick clay-like ground.[10] These mega-cities include Jakarta, Indonesia; Ho Chi Minh, Vietnam; Bangkok, Thailand; Dhaka, Bangladesh; Tokyo, Japan; Venice, Italy; Manila, Philippines; and others.[11]

Even as these changing weather patterns are happening simultaneously across our entire planet, nature does not behave in a linear fashion. We must be more prepared than ever by viewing climate warming as a disaster occurring on a global, planetary scale. Stephen Hawking, the noted scientist and futurist, has already written off Planet Earth. He says we should begin exploring other planets.

Among the objectives of this book is to examine how we might wean ourselves off "a moth to the flame" style of urban planning characterized by the building of large cities near bodies of water even as they are becoming very vulnerable to sea level rise.

A Call to Action is required of all of us, especially of our Millennials and Post Millennials. Central to this call is the development of "Plan Relocation" or "Plan R": the relocation of millions into sustainable, resilient rural communities, large-scale urban developments and high-rise, mega-cities. This Plan Relocation prefigures the comments made by Hawking when he spoke to the Radio Times on the near certainty of planetary disaster prior to his Reith Lecture on black holes.

Although the chance of a disaster to planet Earth in each year may be quite low, it adds up over time, and becomes a near certainty in the next thousand or ten thousand years. However, we will not establish self-sustaining colonies in space for at least the next hundred years, so we have to be very careful in this period.

Stephen Hawking[12]

A PERSPECTIVE ON HISTORY

Many people think that the industrial revolution had its roots in the mid 1800's but the elements of industrialization originated from much earlier times. The architectural historian, Lewis Mumford, in his book *Culture and Cities* found that the seeds of industrialization were planted during the medieval times and its guilds, apprenticeships and system of feudalism. From this perspective, perhaps the so-called "Dark Ages" could not have been so dark if during such times structures like Chartres, the abbey church of Mont St. Michel and cities like Machu Picchu were constructed.

Understanding that our industrial revolution actually draws from a much earlier time is the kind of right-sizing necessary to appreciate our existence as human beings as a tiny speck of time in the history of the earth. Consider the time that cockroaches as a species have been on earth – 360 million years – as compared to that of our ancestors, a mere 6 million years, with humans in our modern form only 200,000 years![13]

A change in perspective also applies in understanding what is happening now. For though the notion of global warming and the associated climate change may be difficult to process, drastic climate changes have been occurring all over the planet in real time as well as throughout the earth's history.

LIMITS TO GROWTH

We also know that for some time others have been warning of the possible limits to growth on this earth. Looking back to the 1970's, members of the Club of Rome[14] – a global think tank established in 1968 – believed that the earth's limited natural resources imposed certain "limits to growth." Their predictions harken back to those made by Thomas Malthus back in 1798, when he indicated that the geometric growth in population would far outpace the arithmetic growth in food supplies.

Malthus calculated that the human population would increase 1 billion people for every 25 years. And considering there were 1 billion people in 1800, Malthus' prediction of a world population of 10 billion by 2025 proved not to be so far off. Our current projections set that figure to about 8.3 billion given an annual world population growth rate of 1.13%.[15] We have heeded neither Malthus' nor the Club of Rome's admonition. Instead with the projected population increase and our continuing consumerism, we continue to strain our earth's natural resources.

Since the 1970's, books like *The Limits to Growth* commissioned by The Club of Rome, *Small is Beautiful* by E.F. Schumacher and *Motivation and Personality* by Abraham Maslow have asked us to look at the impact that our lifestyles have on our environment and the quality of our lives. For these and other valuable resources around "an organic whole" approach to life, see our Bibliography and a summary of Maslow's theory of self-actualization provided in Appendix H.

We believe the ideas outlined in this book may represent the greatest opportunity the private sector will have since modern civilization has evolved. This opportunity lies in establishing a pathway for the relocation of the vast human populations vulnerable to the devastating impact of extreme weather events. Our Plan Relocation – Plan R – envisions accommodating the 1.5 billion more people living on the planet within the next 34 years. We can start with areas of this country and those locations already identified as being climate vulnerable.

THE PRICE OF EXPERIENCE

This book is a blueprint for action. **A Call to Action** is akin to the howling of a dog in wrathful elements; the moaning of a soldier on the battlefield among the happier dead; or when the hungry become the "hangry." In William Blake's poem, *What is the Price of Experience*, 'wisdom is sold in the desolate marketplace where none come to buy."

THE PRICE OF EXPERIENCE

What is the price of Experience? Do men buy it for a song?
Or wisdom for a dance in the street?
No it is bought with the price
Of all that man hath, his house, his wife, his children
Wisdom is sold in the desolate market where none come to buy
And in the wither'd field where the farmer plows for bread in vain.

It is an easy thing to triumph in the summer's sun
And in the vintage and to sing on the waggon loaded with corn

It is an easy thing to talk of patience to the afflicted
To speak the laws of prudence to the homeless
wanderer
To listen to the hungry raven's cry in wintry season
When the red blood is fill'd with wine and with the
marrow of lambs.

It is an easy thing to laugh at wrathful elements
To hear the dog howl at the wintry door, the ox in the
slaughter house moan;
To see a god on every wind and a blessing on every
blast
To hear sounds of love in the thunderstorm that
destroys our enemies' house;
To rejoice in the blight that covers his field and the
sickness that cuts off his children
While our olive and vine sing and laugh round our
door, and our children bring fruits and flowers

Then the groan and the dolor are quite forgotten and
the slave grinding at the mill
And the captive in chains and the poor in the prison
and the soldier in the field
When the shatter'd bone hath laid him groaning among
the happier dead
It is an easy thing to rejoice in the tents of prosperity;
Thus could I sing and thus rejoice: but it is not so
with me.

William Blake 1797[16]

CHAPTER 3
Betting With Our Lives

What signals that this is a unique time in the history of human beings? Consider, with 7.5 billion humans living on earth, simultaneously, many other life forms are starting to disappear. With a population scheduled to grow to 9 billion by 2050, how can we feed ourselves, feed that many more people, as our food chain is being depleted due to the extinction of essential species?

Our reliance on fossil fuels, plastic and the acquisition of things characterize a consumerist and commoditized society that cannot be sustained in its current form.

Eric recalls how his professor of marketing at The Wharton School, Stew Debruicker, reminded his students how every day in business "you bet your career." Here, the stakes are even higher: if we do not come up with effective solutions to the challenge of a growing world population faced with extreme climate change we will have effectively bet with our lives and lost. Given all the evidence that exists, should we be betting with our lives by continuing to debate if and whether climate change is occurring and if it is man-made? What we need now is a new paradigm that deals with the increasing human population, dramatically changing weather patterns and a loss of essential species that reduces our food supply chain and changes our natural ecosystem.

Once again, a change in perspective is in order. If generations before us also had electricity, plumbing and other such modern conveniences, can we say that we are today all that more evolved?   In other words, has the pace of technology allowed us to evolve, or has it been merely feeding our consumerist appetites and playing into our view of a commoditized world? From another point of view, how have our phones and hyperfeed to the Internet made us more intelligent, or enabled us to become creative, thoughtful individuals?

Increasingly the advancement in information technology is outpacing our development as a species. We need our economic framework, our political environment, our psychological viewpoints and our sociological interactions to evolve for us to meet the challenges of our future.

To borrow from Yiddish – EPPES (pronounced *ep-pes*, meaning "a little something") – we need a "little something" different in our **e**conomic, our **p**olitical, our **p**sychological and our **s**ociological perspective to meet the challenges of the future. As our current perspectives in these four areas constrain our ability to work together in addressing climate change, we need an EPPS Shift to occur. We will explore this in Chapter 12.

CHAPTER 4
The Sustainability Movement

The sustainability movement emerged from an increasing awareness of the earth's environment by conservationists, futurists and independent thinkers. We share how their ideas were communicated in print and through popular culture. Increasingly, certain futurists and leading business entrepreneurs see in sustainability the opportunities for financial and economic growth. In this book, we bring together these various strands to strengthen and, in some cases, refocus our market economy towards a sustainable way of life along various dimensions: in the management of our natural resources; the alignment of our financial structures and measurement of business performance; the development and utilization of innovation and technologies to increase energy efficiency; and the establishment of sustainable, resilient communities. You can find more books that cover the relationship between sustainable development and climate resilience in the Bibliography at the end of this book.

Rachel Carson's *Silent Spring* published in 1962 made many aware of the relationship between ecology and conservation. In her seminal book, she documented the harmful effects of certain pesticides on the environment when, back in the day, "ecology" was the precursor to sustainability.

R. Buckminster "Bucky" Fuller – a futurist well beyond his time and even our own time – criticized back in the 1940s the pernicious effect of fossil fuels. Fuller already had the foresight of advocating the use and development of solar energy some sixty years ago. Sad we did not heed his advice back then; perhaps we might have if we only knew then what we know now. Still while knowledge may be a condition for action, it does not follow that even with knowledge we would have taken the right action.

Some may remember the TV commercial of an American Indian in a land filled with garbage. The "tear" on his face registered his disappointment with our society for not respecting and caring for the land. It has been often said we are only custodians of the land where nature is the rightful owner.

Still others foretold our potential future. In 1961, for example, in one episode of the *Twilight Zone* – a series written by science fiction writer Rod Serling – the earth was heating up very quickly because it had changed its orbit and was moving closer to the sun. In *The Midnight Sun*, a young woman, who is a painter and the last person alive in New York City, is dreaming that nighttime temperatures of 110° F are rising to 120° F by mid-day. This proves to be a forewarning of what has been effectively happening with the loss of the earth's ozone layer. Characteristic of the *Twilight Zone*, the episode ends with an awful twist. When she wakes in a fever, it is -10° F. Rather than moving towards the sun, the earth has been moving away from the sun. Deprived of sunlight, the earth will freeze and darkness will prevail.

Too bad Serling smoked four packs of cigarettes a day; he died way too early. It would have been great to have his foresight all these years that he has been gone.

TREE HUGGERS AND CAPITALISTS

The past fifty plus years have seen the emergence of NGOs (non-governmental organizations) like Greenpeace, NRDC, WWF, EDF, Habitat for Humanity and The Nature Conservancy, all of whom are acting as stewards for our resources and species. These NGOs are important for our society as they act as "governors" against harmful developments.

Are "tree huggers" and "capitalists" mutually exclusive? We don't think so. Jigar Shah and Richard Branson are leaders in both camps. Shah founded Sun Edison and sold it for $500 million; he now promotes green capitalism as the wave of the future. Branson of the Virgin Group – Virgin Megastores, Virgin Airlines and Virgin Records – is an adventurer who, as Elizabeth Howell reports, is going to be offering space travel.[17] Bill Gates, one of the titans in the age of computers, has recently expanded his philanthropy to include climate change. Other billionaires like Michael Bloomberg, Jeremy Grantham and Tom Steyer are promoting efforts to address the effects of climate change.

THE TRIPLE BOTTOM LINE

Since the mid-late 19th century, businesses have primarily focused on the "financial" bottom line at the expense of environmental and social costs. This traditional measure does not factor in the full costs of their business activities, their impact on the environment and society.

Businesses who instead account for the triple bottom line measure their performance from all three perspectives: financial, environmental and social. They consider, for example, how they reduce the harmful effects of their activities or contribute in positive ways to the environment. In other words, companies utilizing the triple bottom line are signaling that they value their economic, environmental and social performance.

With the rise in corporate social responsibility (CSR), divisions and departments increasingly report to a c-suite officer – president, chief operating officer or chief executive officer – and observe business standards recommended by organizations like the Coalition for Environmentally Economies (CERES) and the Sustainable Accounting Standards Board.

THE ZEITGEIST MOVEMENT / THE VENUS PROJECT

Peter Joseph is a filmmaker/musician who wrote, directed, narrated, scored and produced the *Zeitgeist* Trilogy – a film series comprised of *Zeitgeist: The Movie* in 2007, *Zeitgeist: Addendum* in 2008 and *Zeitgeist: Moving Forward* in 2011. Joseph prominently featured Jacque Fresco and his Venus Project in *Zeitgeist: Addendum* as being a powerful influence in Joseph's thinking.

Fresco founded the Venus Project 1995 to address "age-old inadequacies of war, poverty, hunger, debt and unnecessary human suffering."[18] Among his solutions, futurist Fresco urged a redesign of culture and society by utilizing forward thinking in sustainable cities, energy efficient practices, natural resource management and automation – operating within a larger framework he called a resource-based society. Eric reframes this approach and renames it as resource capitalism to highlight the vast opportunities for new jobs, economic growth, innovation, local manufacturing and entrepreneurialism that exist with the adoption of a green economy.

RESOURCE CAPITALISM

Fuller once estimated the "true" cost of cheap oil, gas and coal to be a mind boggling $1 million per gallon[19] – a cost that reflects the depletion of and harm to our natural assets of water, air and the ecosystem that allows us to grow food as well as health and occupational risks. During Eric's trip to southern West Virginia in October 2016, when he explored active and abandoned coal-mining towns, he saw how fossil fuel mining has had (and continues to have) a severe impact on air quality, water quality and the ability to grow food.

So how do we move from our current system of finance capitalism to a system that is based on the availability and sustainable use of our natural resources as advocated in the Venus Project and the Zeitgeist Movement? We see that our capitalist and market-based framework can be right-sized by shifting the focus towards safeguarding resources and using the triple bottom line as a mechanism for such policy.

In this way resource capitalism provides a framework for combining the triple bottom line and the green economy, which as a system would reward responsible, sustainable use of resources and promote job growth and long-term economic development.

CHAPTER 5
PLAN B AND CHALLENGES

Lester Brown's Plan B "calls for cutting net carbon dioxide emissions 80 percent by 2020." His objective was to prevent the concentration of carbon dioxide from reaching or exceeding 400 parts per million. But now, global readings of CO_2 levels indicate we have passed 400 ppm as of March 2016.[20] In his *Plan B 3.0: Mobilizing to Save Civilization*, he urges the following measures.[21]

> First, investing in energy efficiency will allow us to keep global energy demand from increasing. Then we can cut carbon emissions by one third by replacing fossil fuels with renewable energy sources for electricity and heat production. A further 14 percent drop comes from restructuring our transportation systems and reducing coal and oil use in industry. Ending net deforestation worldwide can cut CO_2 emissions another 16 percent. Last, planting trees and managing soils to sequester carbon can absorb 17 percent of our current emissions.

THE GREEN ECONOMY

The green economy aims to reduce environmental risks and ecological scarcities as it strives for sustainable development. The 2011 UNEP Green Economy Report establishes "that to be green, an economy must not only be efficient, but also fair. Fairness implies recognising global and country level equity dimensions, particularly in assuring a just transition to an economy that is low-carbon, resource efficient, and socially inclusive."[22]

As such the green economy is distinct from prior economic systems as it recognizes natural capital and the economic value of ecological services. It does this by requiring all costs generated by the company's activities be included and counted as external costs and liabilities of the company when such activities harm or adversely affect society and its ecosystems.[23]

Consider how the diagram on the following page for Sustainable Development presents a fuller accounting of a company's operations on the economy, the environment and society. This triple bottom line perspective contrasts with the economic performance metric companies traditionally use to measure their operations and success. When they report a good year of economic performance to the company management and their shareholders, they do not capture the full impact of their operations. The public may be, instead, suffering from the company's operations when they adversely affect the quality of life, clean air, clean water and food supplies where these companies operate. Under this limited measurement, the public would not be compensated for such losses.

SUSTAINABLE DEVELOPMENT DIAGRAM[24]

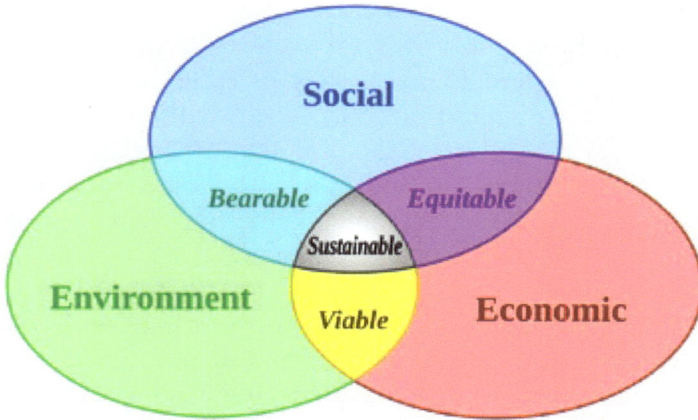

Judging from the some 400,000 people who participated in the climate march in New York City in September 2014, the green economy is here. And there are more indications.

LOCAL, NATIONAL AND GLOBAL AGENDA

Cities like New York City are taking real steps toward the establishment of a green economy. NYC has set a goal of reducing carbon emissions by 80% by that magic year 2050. Still it remains unclear how we will accomplish even these goals if we don't have a viable renewable energy strategy for high-rise structures in densely populated areas. So far it appears that some northeastern and midwestern cities (even sustainable-friendly New York) may be settling for the easier option of switching from coal and oil to natural gas, from a dirtier to a relatively "cleaner" source. This appears implied when we hear that some say natural gas is a "necessary transitional fuel" even though natural gas, too, is a fossil fuel.

At The NRF / Built Environment, we encourage our city officials and council members not to settle for just a shift from oil to gas. We can do better with technologies like cogeneration / trigeneration that also increase energy efficiency. Cogeneration provides both heat and power while trigeneration (through the use of chillers) offers heating, power and cooling. So while cogen and trigen still utilize natural gas as a relatively cleaner fossil fuel, these systems recapture half of the energy or "waste heat" generated to create electricity. Instead of losing this half to the atmosphere, this energy is recycled to generate heat and, with the use of chillers, cooling. Finally, in cases of power outages, these cogens and trigens can incorporate resilience features such as continuous power availability, black start and island-mode to protect large buildings from going off-line or being forced to use gas generators that are even more polluting.

COGENERATOR PLANT
MANUFACTURED BY INTELLIGEN POWER SYSTEMS[25]

In the U.S., our legislators remain divided over climate change: between the Democratic party starting to advocate an 80% carbon footprint reduction by the year 2050 and the Republican party, in turn divided between its moderates and extremists over the role that human activity plays in global warming and its effect on climate change. Some Republicans even deny the existence of climate change. But even if our leaders were unanimous in acknowledging the role of human activity and committed to action, it remains to be seen whether we can achieve such objectives without some re-thinking of our socio-political and, even, financial structures.

The Paris Agreement / COP21 of December 2015 is historic but its objectives may not be realized in time. It was a historic achievement to secure a worldwide consensus to globally reduce carbon emissions. But whether such reductions and objectives can be achieved under the current structures will be as Eric's professor, Debruicker, uttered – a bet made with our lives. See Appendix A for a summary of the major points of the Paris Agreement.

In any case, developed economies will all have to make serious compromises to become less reliant on fossil fuels. Our developed economies will also have to acknowledge the unfair advantage we have had with the use of fossil fuels over developing countries. Having to play catch up, they are now being urged to reduce their use of fossil fuels, which was a primary driver for development in the past. The concept of "reparations" from the developed world to the developing world goes some distance in addressing this unfair advantage as well as providing a down payment for these countries to develop and utilize sustainable technologies and renewable energy sources for their economies. The NRF has been advocating certain financing strategies such as investment tax credits to help generate the $100B USD annual payment by developed countries to developing ones starting 2020 as part of the Paris Agreement / COP21.

CARBON TAXING IN A CORPORATOCRACY

Several countries, including Sweden, Finland, Great Britain, British Colombia and Chile, already have implemented some form of taxation on carbon emissions.[26] Perhaps this is why during the 2015 Paris Agreement nearly half of the national pledges submitted referenced carbon pricing.

In the United States, we face the challenge that our large companies, including ones with an interest in, related to, or affiliated with fossil fuel industries, have strong lobbies working to block attempts to establish carbon taxation. This occurred in 2010, when the Obama Administration tried to legislate some form of carbon taxation with disastrous results.

Political interests are increasingly now aligned with large corporate interests rather than traditional party lines. Corporations are hiring lobbying groups to promote the corporate perspective and influence legislation favoring corporate interests. As a result our current U.S. political system is becoming more of a corporatocracy[27] than an actual democracy. This evolution of our political system is one of the reasons for the growing vast inequities between the so-called "1% and the other 99%."

For this reason, we have avoided discussions about carbon taxation, although our NRF co-founder, James-Robert Sellinger, remains enthusiastic about such a tax. Perhaps with conservative and influential thinkers, like Hank Paulson who continues to advocate for carbon taxation to reduce our carbon emissions, there may be hope for this strategy sometime in the future.

We do believe in encouraging the private sector through subsidies and investment tax credits so they invest in carbon reducing activities. See Appendix B at the end of this book for a summary of The NRF's White Paper and the NRF's other activities on the company website.[28]

Carbon taxation along with Brown's Plan B of a green economy will reorient current practices towards creating green jobs and reducing our collective carbon footprint through recycling, reusing, repurposing and relying on renewable energy technologies. This is a pathway out of a spiraling cycle of rising temperatures, changing weather patterns and the rising of the seas.

OUR DEPENDENCY ON PLASTIC

Among the reasons why our civilization is not sustainable in its current form is our reliance on plastic. Many everyday products are manufactured with a least some portion of plastic. Plastic does not decompose or biodegrade; it accumulates in our landfills; pollutes our environment; and damages our ecosystems.

Jessica Knoblauch of Environmental Health News, for example, noted how "plastic debris, laced with chemicals . . . can injure or poison wild life . . . . floating plastic waste which can survive for thousands of years in water, serve as mini transportation devices for invasive species, disrupting habitats . . . . [and] plastic buried deep in landfills can leach harmful chemicals that spread into groundwater."

The design of plastic can be traced to the year 1907.

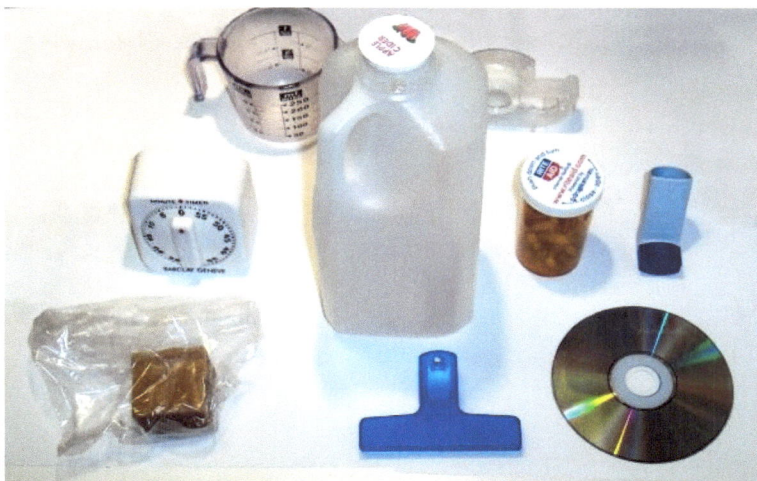

Some household items made of various types of plastic.[29]

Plastic is a material consisting of any of a wide range of synthetic or semi-synthetic organic compounds that are malleable and can be molded into solid objects. Plastics are typically organic polymers of high molecular mass, but they often contain other substances. They are usually synthetic, most commonly derived from petrochemicals, but many are made from renewable materials such as polylactic acid from corn or cellulosic from cotton linters...

Due to their relatively low cost, ease of manufacture, versatility, and imperviousness to water, plastics are used in an enormous and expanding range of products, from paper clips to spaceships. They have already displaced many traditional materials, such as wood, stone, horn, and bone, leather, paper, metal, glass and ceramic, in most of their former uses. In developed countries, about a third of plastic is used in packaging and another

Third in buildings such as piping used in plumbing or vinyl siding. Other uses include automobiles (up to 20% plastic), furniture, and toys. In the developing world, the ratios may be different - for example, reportedly 42% of India's plastic consumption is used in packaging. Plastics have many uses in the medical field as well, to include polymer implants, however the field of plastic surgery is not named for use of plastic material, but rather the more generic meaning of the word plasticity in regards to the reshaping of flesh…

The success and dominance of plastics starting in the early 20th century led to environmental concerns regarding its slow decomposition rate after being discarded as trash due to its composition of very large molecules. Toward the end of the century, one approach to this problem was met with wide efforts toward recycling.[30]

Inside the Garbage of the World, documentary filmmaker, Phillipe Carillo, conveyed how harmful our use and disposal of plastic is to the ecosystem and oceans. Now every time Eric is in a store he brings his own bag or carries his stuff without a bag. But he notices that most check-out assistants automatically start "bagging" things in plastic bags. So when he requests, "no bag please," he finds most have to stop and shift within a split second from their mechanical, thought pattern to not bag the items.

WHO IS RUNNING THE SHIP?

This shift towards a resource-based economy, to institute the green economy on a large scale, promote sustainability and build resiliency requires "leadership" and collective action. But without any one really "running the ship," corporatocracies and other influencers resist these advances in favor of their short-term profits.

CHAPTER 6
A NEW INDUSTRY:
CLIMATE RESILIENCE

Resilience can be understood as the ability to withstand a shock efficiently, effectively and to bounce back to a previous state of equilibrium. Carefully thought-out resilient measures have the added benefit of improving the situation even after the event. We would characterize climate resilience as measures that protect or enable us to effectively and efficiently rebound back from the effects of extreme weather events. Climate resilience is something we need to develop as the frequency and intensity of extreme weather events is increasing worldwide.

THREAT MULTIPLIERS

Our colleague, Steve Wilson, informed us that increasingly the military is concerned about how climate change can multiply threats or create threat multipliers that may even threaten national security. For example, what may start as a severe drought in an area results in the threat of inadequate quantities of food and water. The extreme agitation people experience then further escalates into their fighting with each other over the limited essential resources. This aggression when further intensified by clashes over perhaps cultural or religious beliefs can make the area, even the region, a hotbed for terrorism that the military would view as a national security threat.

The existence of such threat multipliers resulting from extreme weather events may further require military presence in the affected area for any number of reasons such as maintaining order, distributing essential food and water supplies, and relocating individuals.

The Hoover Dam, Nevada, USA Light-colored rock indicates previous water levels within the dam due to drought. Source: Arlen Stawasz

These disaster recovery situations are multiplying across the globe in "real time." The frequency and severity of these situations point to the urgency of changing our perspective and our approach to dealing with both the disaster and the causes of the disaster. Disaster, which if not properly addressed or better yet avoided, can become a potent force, unleashing political, religious and other social unrest.

Taking actions that allow us to cope with or even avoid climate related disaster requires the force of will and equivalent power that Franklin Delano Roosevelt utilized during the Great Depression. FDR utilized his powers to quickly and unilaterally approve investments in large-scale infrastructure on a level never realized before in this country. His foresight allowed the U.S. to mobilize for World War II when all industries shifted focus to one directed goal, winning the war.

Today we must mobilize in a different way, not to wage a war, but to prepare for climate related disaster. We can also mobilize in adopting and taking actions to, as this book advocates and discusses, establish a green economy, mandate the triple bottom line for all companies, and shift to a resource-based framework. Perhaps then with all these actions, instituted collectively within the U.S. and around the world, we can slow down or stop the increase in global warming. We can no longer view climate change and all the threats it poses from an "us versus them" mentality. Rather we require a global perspective on how to best allocate our renewable and non-renewable resources and find a mechanism that more equitably distributes the wealth generated from these resources.

MOVING WITH NATURE

Penguins, whales and seals are relocating to more hospitable climates. Bodies of water are literally drying up. Damaging winds in certain locations are signaling their change to desert conditions. Still other areas face alternating patterns of frequent flooding and droughts. These and many other events establish that human beings are not stronger than nature; and rather than working against or defending against nature we should be working with nature.

A lot of precious energy and resources have been expended debating about the impacts we have created and funding studies undertaken by a host of think tanks, NFPs, NGOs and governmental agencies. From the Latin phrase *"caveat emptor,"* we caution those to beware of those studies that minimize the effects of climate change. Rather than more studies, debates and lobbying, we should be directing our valuable resources, efforts and, most importantly, time to preparing ourselves and protecting our swelling human population worldwide from the effects of extreme weather events with, for example, sustainable and resilient housing and green infrastructure.

We say, let's "seize the day" – *carpe diem* in Latin – for the day is all we have in front of us. All the meetings, reports, discussions and so forth can be put aside to create something of value for our species.

To illustrate our point, as Joaquin was in the last stages of editing this book, he learned from his daily read of the *New York Times* that residents in Princeville, North Carolina, having been battered by Hurricane Floyd in 1999, faced Hurricane Matthew just recently in October 2016. The "water pouring around a levee built around the Tar River and into the town, inundating hundreds of homes,"[31] was one of two floods to have occurred within 17 years. This area that was in a 100-year flood zone was supposed to have a one-percent or greater chance of experiencing flood in any single year. Of the 750 single-family homes, 241 were very seriously damaged while another 241 were still quite damaged.

These town residents may again have the choice they were given in 1999 to sell their homes to the Federal Emergency Management Agency (FEMA). They rejected that option in 1999 believing it would mean the end of their community – a town that traces its establishment in 1865 to the freed slave, Turner Prince. It became home to many African-Americans. We anticipate by the time this book is published, their town commissioners will have voted on whether to make available to homeowners the FEMA buyout option, or again request the levee to be fixed as well as secure financial assistance to repair their homes. We hope the amounts provided by FEMA are sufficient to allow them to reconstruct their homes on elevated support foundations and incorporate other resiliency measures.

It is becoming clear, whether like a slow trickle or a tsunami, people in climate-affected areas will increasingly have to relocate. As painful as this decision will be, the government – on the federal, state and local levels – must step-up for these relocations to occur in a planned, coherent fashion. This will require a framework for public, private and community partnerships and providing the necessary financial incentives and resources.

Among those displaced from the effects of the flooding along the rivers of Bangladesh.
Source: Arlen Stawasz

CHAPTER 7
PARTS TO A WHOLE:
SUSTAINABILITY AND RESILIENCY

Many of us "silo" sustainability and resilience as exclusive and separate categories. Their inter-dependent nature, however, really forms "an organic whole." Eric developed this viewpoint from his experience as CFO and co-founder of a large public-private partnership with the City of New York to conceive, develop, build and operate a large observation wheel on Staten Island – The New York Wheel.[32]

Climate resilience as applied to this project involved considering the risks inherent in a built environment located in a flood zone. Facing sea level rise or SLR was a real possibility as the project has a 99-year lease with the City of New York. Scientists project that the SLR in this area during the next 100 years could be anywhere from 2-6 feet (0.5 to 2 meters+/-).

Staten Island, New York City, NY. Rendering of New York Wheel.

A sustainable and climate resilient design of The New York Wheel required Eric to understand the interaction between the impact of this project on the environment as well as the effect of extreme weather events on the project. He saw the importance of integrating at the early design stage the kinds of sustainable and resilient features listed below.

Key Elements when Designing Sustainable and Resilient Projects New York Wheel

o Move mechanical systems out of flood zones or at least flood-proof them;

o Incorporate storm water management design;

o Create green roofs and urban greening features;

o Build to LEED Certification standards;

o Use alternative energies, rather than fossil fuels.

Guided by this experience, later when we formed The NRF as a public charity in 2013, Joaquin and James-Robert along with David Gibson – a well-regarded architect and early adopter of energy efficiency – developed a checklist of ten high value features to "protect, enhance and preserve" the built environment. These are included in the summary of our White Paper in Appendix B at the end of this book.

In order to carry out and implement sustainability and resiliency as an integrated solution we also need to address the challenge of financing, reorienting public-private partnerships around the community, instituting a clearer and more definitive process for decision-making, and enlisting expert professional resources.

CRACKING THE FINANCING NUT

We established The NRF in response to the concerns raised by community leaders who met in lower Manhattan following Superstorm Sandy. This hurricane devastated much of the coastal sections of lower Manhattan, Brooklyn and Staten Island on September 29, 2012.

Among our objectives at The NRF was to develop and advocate for large-scale financing for the scale of resiliency infrastructure needed to "protect, enhance and preserve" the homes where residents live, the offices operated by businesses and the delivery of essential public services to them both.

Quite early on we realized that resilience initiatives such as flood-proofing and hardening infrastructure would be very difficult to finance under conventional practices. Lenders as well as investors and owners want to know how long or how many years it will take before their investment is paid back either from the revenue generated; or, as we emphasize the anticipated savings from not having to undertake repairs when the investments made allowed them to avoid or reduce the level of damage that could have been caused by weather events if they had done nothing. This time period is called the payback period.

Consider, for example, how Joaquin determined his payback period in deciding whether he and his partner should install solar panels at their home in Brooklyn. The system would cost them about $14,000, which they would have to pay up-front. The total value of federal, state and local tax incentives was $13,300 – an amount they could later use to reduce their personal and property taxes. This made their net cost after tax credits: $700. Based on a two-year history of their ConEdison electric bill, they projected an average reduction in their monthly electric bill of $100. After finding it would take them seven months to "pay back" their net costs; they signed up.

Determining the payback period in resiliency projects is more complex primarily because we do not know with certainty when an extreme and devastating climate-related event will occur. We also do not know how severe the impact will be. But we can substitute certainties with formulas that consider the probabilities of extreme weather events occurring in an area and project their cost based on past and modeled future occurrences.

An alternative payback calculation is based on the evidence of a $4 return to every $1 invested for resiliency infrastructure. FEMA learned that a municipality would enjoy a four-fold benefit from the amount invested in resiliency measures, again, in the form of future savings from repairs to, or avoiding a loss of, property resulting from a weather event in the unforeseeable future.[33]

TAX CREDITS AND SUBSIDIES

It was during a seminar on resilience in April 2013[34] that Eric thought why not reconfigure investment tax credits and use them as one way to finance climate resilience.

Investment tax credits (ITCs) have been quite effective since the early 1960's to stimulate investment in diverse areas as alternative energy, historic real estate rehabilitation, motion pictures and, even, hiring people (in a related program called the earned income tax credit). Every dollar invested in these activities had the additional virtue of generating, what economists call, a multiplier effect, where every dollar invested generates a multiple of three to five dollars of new economic benefits. If properly structured and planned, these benefits can go to the community where the project utilizing the tax credit is located, providing that community with new jobs that employ its residents, which in turn allow them to spend locally and support local businesses.

Based on this notion of ITCs, Eric conceptualized as one of The NRF's original financing strategies the creation of two funds: the Climate Resilience Investment Tax Credit Fund (CR-ITC Fund) and, a companion program, the Climate Resilience Investment Subsidy Fund (CRIS Fund). From the large pool of money generated through such tax credits, the CR-ITC Fund would provide a grant of about 10-20% of the cost of large-scale resiliency projects undertaken by public-private partnerships, public, private and community partnerships, or by municipalities.

Using a similar concept, but this time funded from a small levy on insurance and utility companies, the CRIS Fund would provide financial subsidies to owners making their large-scale properties sustainable and resilient. We believe it would be in the business interests of these utility and insurance companies to support resiliency projects and provide these subsidies to owners as such sustainable, resilient measures would help protect their utilities and reduce the amount of payouts and repairs by these insurance and utility companies.

On the federal level, the CR-ITC involves a front-end benefit to any investor where a federal tax credit matches the amount of the original investment. If the state where the investor resides or files company taxes similarly provides a CR-ITC, the investor would receive an additional reduction in state taxes. This additional reduction effectively operates as a one-time return on investment. This concept allows for the investor to recoup the investment but when the state also participates, the investor then realizes a return. This relieves the pressure on the resilience project to achieve the kinds of investment returns typically expected in other kinds of investments. This structure is not unlike the real estate tax shelter syndications of the 1980s that stimulated billions of dollars of investment in real estate.

For example, should an investor invest $25 in an eligible climate resilience project, that investor would receive back the amount in the form of a federal investment tax credit to then be used or applied to reduce the investor's personal or business tax liability. While the investor is front-loading the financing of the project, the investor can be made largely whole by the next tax year assuming the federal tax credit allows a dollar for dollar credit. And if the state offers a similar tax credit, say 50% of the invested amount, our investor would be given $12.50 from the state to reduce the investor's state tax. The total $37.50 in total tax credits, thus, returns the principal of the investor's investment and allows a one-time 50% return.

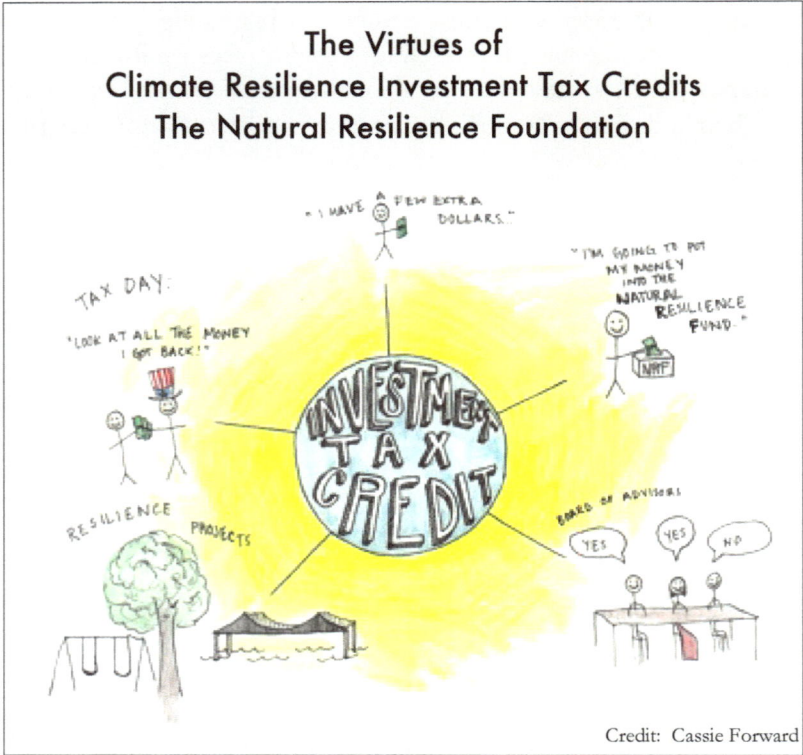

The Virtues of
Climate Resilience Investment Tax Credits
The Natural Resilience Foundation

Credit: Cassie Forward

We envision that many large public infrastructure projects with a resiliency component can be financed under a 90/10 or 80/20 offered under the CR-ITC model. Here the municipality is reasonably expected to come up with 10-20%, which it could provide by tapping into the proceeds of the CR-ITC Fund. The municipality could finance the remainder through long-term debt having an interest rate reflective of the level of risk in the project. For example, interest in less risky debt might be 2-3% in today's low interest rate environment and higher risk debt would be anywhere from 4% to 10%. Private property owners would similarly apply to the CRIS Fund for a subsidy around 10% of the project cost.

THE S+R PARADIGM

From this paradigm, we pair sustainability with resiliency so we can use the dollars saved from energy-saving measures and renewable energy technologies (the sustainability part of the equation) to help finance resiliency measures. Eric developed this financing concept during a brainstorming session with David Gibson.

Some financial institutions are already using the cost savings projected under certain energy-saving programs to finance such investments. These include property assessed clean energy (PACE), green bonds and power purchase agreements (PPAs). Such programs allow property owners to replace heating, ventilation and air conditioning systems with no front-end cost. The government offers subsidies for these improvements.

Though the cost savings under these lease-based PPAs are less than an outright purchase of the system, the building does get an upgrade and more sustainable/resilient energy solution with no out-of-pocket cost. These types of financing mechanisms are very much needed for property owners who do not have the capital to purchase these systems. Refinancing their properties to wrap-around these improvements can be complex and require lenders to be creative on issues as securing their interest in the improvements. Homeowners who have equity built up in their homes can also access home equity lines of credit.

ADDING COMMUNITY TO PUBLIC-PRIVATE PARTNERSHIPS

Some estimates indicate that $90 trillion dollars will be required for new infrastructure by the Year 2050.[35] President Trump's interest in launching a federal plan to invest one trillion in infrastructure,[36] if towards sustainable and resilient infrastructure would be a significant step in this direction. It is likely this plan will involve public-private partnerships.

Often such PPPs as they are commonly known, distinguish the interests of the "public" from those of the private sector. This distinction treats as a monolithic group the interests of any number of "public" stakeholders including various levels of the government, non-profits, community and advocacy organizations, and residents whether as a group or as individuals. The private interests tend to refer to the financial, real estate and investment sectors. Within this framework, the interests of the community and the location where the project or investment is to occur are often lost in the larger discussion of public entitlements (a catchall for government incentives, subsidies and other benefits).

From another perspective, PPPs tend to focus, on the financial, physical and revenue-generating aspects of a project, this being the financing of "bricks and mortar" and the realization of a profit. This view again discounts the impact on the community, on the residents and how their needs and interests might be better met through, for example, a combination of "bricks and mortar" and accompanying programs and services to ensure access, information and equity. Such programs that rethink and deliver workforce development (in the areas of retraining, skill preparation and candidate presentation as well as addressing background checks) and local employment are sorely needed.

For this reason, we believe, by developing Public, Private and Community Partnerships – that we call PuPCos – we acknowledge the relationship, interdependence and value of these "three" sectors. Private capital, technical capacity and development expertise would promote public policy interests;

and public incentives would reduce the risks associated with and the costs of financing. But the resources of both the private and public sectors would be brought to bear in serving and promoting the community as the end-user.

It is the community of people who drives demand. And it is the community that increasingly wants to participate. Through traditional, social media and digital platforms, individuals are empowered to make known their opinions, needs and interests as well as influence the direction of a project by, for example, supporting a new project, or not, or even actively voicing their resistance.

Private investors, on the other hand, require some way to recover their cost through means like the CR-ITC as well as a stream of returns. The return made possible by the state's participation in the tax credit is a one-time return utilized against the investor's expected taxes. The return or revenue stream, however, is different as it is an annual income an investor expects to receive while the investment remains in the project. Such a stream of revenue may only be generated when there is a real estate component wrapped into or made a part of the project. And more times than not, it is the profitable real estate component that drives the deal rather than the resiliency portion.

Another shot of the reconstructed World Trade Center, through the windows of Brookfield Place Office Complex. Source: Eric Kaufman (2016)

New York City explored two related concepts – the Seaport City[37] and Battery Park City East – that could provide a resiliency embankment (or multi-purpose levee) to protect the Lower East Side of Manhattan. New communities of thousands of housing units, schools, hospitals, offices, hotels and other facilities would be built on this landfill embankment – creating enormous revenue-producing opportunities from residential sales and rentals, and office and commercial properties. These related concepts might still not be feasible as experts more thoroughly examine the effect of sea level rise, which is why the Army Corps of Engineers is also exploring permanent flood barriers as found in Rotterdam, The Netherlands.

Another challenge is that large-scale projects of such a scale will require extensive environmental, land-use, permitting and approval processes of five years or so, which would probably double the period needed for design and planning.

As it stands, we find that the public and private sectors still resist making physical resiliency investments to their built environment. More typically government officials, property owners and real estate managers and developers do not fully understand, have not evaluated nor factored in the risks of climate change and the impact of extreme weather events on their properties, current investments and planned projects. See Appendix E for what a more thorough cost-benefit analysis should include.

As a result, for example, when they upgrade their utility and power systems, they do not take steps to strengthen their resiliency by building in "N+1 redundancy." In this concept, N refers to the existing system, be it a power system or such, where the +1 indicates one backup system to that power system, +2 referring to two backup systems, and so forth. Facilities providing essential services like hospitals or highly sensitive information like financial service institutions may require this type of redundancy.

For these and other reasons (including sea level rise), we advocate the planning and establishment of communities in which to relocate people in facing possible imminent danger. These relocation cities and communities can be seeded with the funding generated from climate resilience tax credits and climate resilience subsidies once lawmakers establish them. We also would incorporate the community by understanding their needs during the critical concept and design stage of planning.

WHO DECIDES?

In the aftermath of Super Storm Sandy, many meetings attended by affected landowners and politicians were stymied by the "chicken and egg" dilemma. Politicians were looking for direction from constituents, while community residents and business owners were looking to these politicians to provide solutions.

We distinguish between two kinds of leadership for the crisis / concept stage and the implementation stage. During the period of crisis leading up to the development of an action or concept, leadership must be able to communicate the need for a particular action and then manage the exchange of ideas and dialogue so that a vision emerges. Bringing those community residents, government officials and business and property owners together for a "meeting of the minds" is vital at this stage. But merely including everyone at that table is not going to generate the vision and mandate necessary for large-scale action.

Once leadership allows that vision to develop and we enter the implementation stage, leadership style must be of a type that allows for timely and effective implementation. Effective implementation will require setting the direction for the public, private and community sectors working in partnership. More times than not, so-called public presentations are poorly managed generally because the benefits to the community have not been adequately considered or such benefits have not been effectively communicated.

Our numerous meetings with different branches of the U.S. federal government provided us with a different challenge: navigating through big government. Pair up the U.S. federal government with a large state like New York and a large city like New York City, you end up with a bureaucrat's dream or a Kafkaesque nightmare, depending on your perspective. This bureaucratic challenge is also experienced in other states and cities as issues of jurisdiction or "turf" battles.

ADVISORS AND CONSULTANTS

During both stages – coming to a meeting of the minds as well as implementing relocation communities – a strong team of advisors and consultants will make a big difference. A blend of new thinking and best practices along with an eye to feasibility is needed for these efforts to stand the test of time for our millennials and post-millennials.

Among the expertise that this team should have include climate resiliency and sustainability and the established practices of economic, real estate and community development, architecture, engineering and transportation. We also see a need for experts and thinkers who understand the social and behavioral impact of living in these newly established or repurposed relocation communities. They must factor in the effect on residents, a wide range of businesses (small and large ones alike) and service delivery establishments like hospitals.

Our shift towards a resource-based, non-fossil fuel-based economy will require specialized consultancies like the Global Climate Adaptation Partnership or GCAP. Founded by Tom Downing, a pioneer of climate adaptation for nearly forty years, his firm has experts like Carmen Lacambra, a trained biologist and humanitarian. Carmen brings a blend and wealth of experiences with her professional practices being in Oxford, England; Austin, Texas; and Bogota, Colombia.[38] Here is their mission.

The earth's climate is changing and will continue to change for decades regardless of any greenhouse gas emissions controls adopted in the future that will continue adversely our lives (threats to water supply, supply chains and environmental deterioration as examples).

Across the world, response is typically divided into two interlinked components: mitigation and adaptation. Mitigation describes the need to reduce greenhouse gas emissions and minimize the changes ahead. Adaptation, on the other hand, is used to describe the fact that further climate change is inevitable and mankind would do well to prepare now for the climate of the future.

Adaptation in its broadest sense is the primary focus of GCAP because in practice most organizations (both public and private) need support to implement appropriate adaptation solutions to minimize the negative impacts of adverse impacts of changing climate.

Our mission is to passionately provide our clients with expert insight into the effects of climate change on their citizens, on their environments, and on their businesses; and to assist our clients in taking proactive steps to develop sustainable and best-value adaptation solutions to their unique climate change challenges.

CHAPTER 8
THE CLOCK IS TICKING

For some time now, we assumed that our valuable natural resources were infinite, when, in fact, many of them are not. Fi-
nite resources include many of the precious minerals we use,
the soil into which we grow our food, the fresh water we drink
and the clean air we breathe. We have relied on artificially
cheap fossil fuels to spur our automobile-centric and consump-
tion-based society in ways that have depleted our resources and
degraded our environment.

For our part, we recognize those pioneers who have persevered
in raising the awareness about the impact that human activity is
having on the earth and climate change. Just a few years ago,
some 400,000 in New York City participated in a global climate
march on September 2014 to protest against a lack of action by
our leaders, corporations and naysayers. They were joined by
similar marches in Berlin, Germany; Bogotá, Colombia; New
Delhi, India; Istanbul, Turkey; Johannesburg, South Africa;
Alawusa, Lagos; London, England; Melbourne, Australia; Paris,
France; and Rio de Janeiro, Brazil.

ExxonMobil (Exxon), one of the world's largest fossil fuel companies, is alleged to have said, "none of its assets were 'stranded' because the impacts of climate change, if any, were uncertain and far off in the future."[39] A class action filed in federal court during November, 2016 provides that Exxon "misled its investors and the public by failing to disclose the risks posed to its business by climate change" and that such failure of disclosure resulted in "stockholders paying inflated prices for Exxon Stock."[40]

Maybe it was the combination of this class action, the on-going SEC investigations, the drop in stock and public action, that caused Exxon to now state on its website that it, too, is concerned with climate change. The following, at least on paper, lays out their strategy for reducing greenhouse gas emissions.

> We have the same concerns as people everywhere – and that is how to provide the world with the energy it needs while reducing greenhouse gas emissions.
>
> The risk of climate change is clear and the risk warrants action. Increasing carbon emissions in the atmosphere are having a warming effect. There is a broad scientific and policy consensus that action must be taken to further quantify and assess the risks.
>
> ExxonMobil is taking action by reducing greenhouse gas emissions in its operations, supporting research that leads to technology breakthroughs and participating in dialogue on policy options.
>
> Addressing climate change, providing economic opportunity and lifting billions out of poverty are complex

and interrelated issues requiring complex solutions. There is a consensus that comprehensive strategies are needed to respond to these risks.

ExxonMobil[41]

Adding to Exxon's public posture, *Climate News Network* reports how a collection of U.S.- and foreign-based fossil-fuel corporations are increasing their investment in renewables and clean energy. They see that Exxon, Shell, Total and Statoil are, among various activities, forming new company divisions, or purchasing other companies, or stepping up their research activities. Some of them are spending individually $1 billion or so. Still "as a proportion of their overall spending, the oil giants' investment in re-newables are still very low, and are dwarfed by their spending on fossil fuel-related activities."[42]

TECHNICAL SOLUTIONS

At this very moment if our young, bright and inquisitive minds in high school are asked to imagine and think through the development of alternative energy sources and energy efficiency stratagems, they may help us find ways to slow down the pace of climate change or soften its impact. Organizations like Alliance for Climate Education are educating young people on the science of climate change and, importantly, are generating their interest in science, technology, engineering and math (also known as STEM) as a pathway for their future.[43]

We have one such example in Andrew Ma, currently a college undergraduate who developed a method for extracting ammonia from wastewater. He received recognition for his scientific achievements during his high school years. As of this writing, in his sophomore year at Princeton, he continues his energy/environmental research.

BIOFUELS

Certain crops, non-food crops, waste biomass and even algae can be converted to generate fuel. First-generation biofuels utilize a process of fermentation to convert crops like sugar (sugarcane and sugarbeet) and starch (corn and sorghum) to form bioalcohols such as ethanol, butanol and propanol. Second-generation biofuels are made from cellulose, found in non-food crops and waste biomass such as corn stover, corncobs, straw, wood, and wood byproducts – and for this reason they are also known as cellulosic biofuels. Third-generation biofuels use algae though they are not yet produced commercially.[44]

For sure there are pros and cons to biofuels. Farmers can generate additional income. But we are seeing that to produce such biofuels, our land, water and air resources are being strained and, in some cases, the level of greenhouse gas emissions can be greater. For these reasons, Eric remains unconvinced that the energy required to produce these first-generation biofuels is much better than fossil fuels. The current method of making biofuel from corn into ethanol seems to be cannibalizing our food supply and, given the growth of our worldwide population, food supplies are an important valued resource. Utilizing crops for fuel is not the answer.

CARBON SEQUESTRATION AND STORAGE

Hoesung Lee, Chair of the IPCC lays out below what milestones must be met in order to address climate warming and some of the technologies needed to do this like carbon sequestration.   The IPCC (Intergovernmental Panel on Climate Change) is a coalition of 1,000 scientists charged with projecting the effects of climate change on our planet.

Carbon sequestration and storage (CSS), also known as carbon capture and storage, is a two-part process that involves capturing the carbon emissions from a source, then burying it into the ground and capping it so the carbon will not escape into the atmosphere.   As Mr. Lee admonishes below there is still much to learn about CSS: its operational safety, the risks of transporting sequestered CO_2 and the long-term integrity of storage.

A TIME FOR SOLUTIONS

With a global consensus that man-made global warming presents a perilous threat to the planet, how do we go about curbing temperature rises and creating a zero-carbon global economy?

Undoubtedly, 2015 was a landmark year in the global development agenda.   Not only did the international community agree to the Sustainable Development Goals (SDGs), but also, to the surprise of some doubters, nations came together at the 21st Conference of the Parties (COP21) to the UN Framework Convention on Climate Change (UNFCCC) in Paris to reach an ambitious and wide-ranging agreement on tackling climate change.

Climate action is, of course, one of the 17 SDGs, and underpins many of the others.   But in this article I would like to concentrate on the Paris Agreement, and what its implementation will mean for sustainable development. In particular I would like to look at the work of the Intergovernmental Panel on Climate Change (IPCC), as the world now seeks to turn climate action into reality.

As the leading world body for the assessment of the science related to climate change, its impacts and possible future risks, and options for dealing with it, the IPCC was a significant contributor to the successful outcome of COP21. The Paris Agreement is based on science, and reflects the findings of past IPCC assessments.

Moreover, COP21 gave an important role to the IPCC, whose future reports will inform the 'global stocktake' process whereby nations monitor their progress towards the goal of limiting global warming to well below 2°C above preindustrial levels and their efforts to limit the temperature increase to 1.5°C.

Our last report, the Fifth Assessment Report, found that to limit warming to below 2°C would require substantial reductions in emissions of greenhouse gases (GHGs) over the next few decades and near-zero emissions of CO_2 and other long-lived GHGs by the end of the century.

To be precise, to have a likely (i.e. two thirds or more) chance of holding warming to 2°C, global emissions in 2050 would have to be 40–70 per cent lower relative to 2010, and net emissions of GHGs would approach zero by 2100. That implies that in 35 years we will have seen a rapid improvement in energy efficiency, and a tripling to quadrupling of the share of zero and low carbon energy supply from renewables, nuclear and legacy fossil fuel, combined with carbon capture and storage (CCS), technology in which carbon emissions are sequestered at the source (e.g. a power plant) and then stored safely, for instance underground.

Workers plant mangrove trees as a conservation garden in Jakarta, Indonesia to mark Earth Day 2009. Source: Dadang

There was less knowledge available at the time of the Fifth Assessment Report about the pathways that would take us to warming of only 1.5°C. The limited number of studies indicates pathways characterised by immediate mitigation and faster reduction of GHG emissions, including the use of negative emissions (withdrawing CO2 from the atmosphere, for instance through technology or afforestation).

The barriers to a zero-carbon society do not arise in

science. We already know enough to hold warming to 2°C, global enough to take action on the path to a carbon-free economy, and that was one of the key messages of the Fifth Assessment Report in 2013/2014 and of its predecessor, the Fourth Assessment Report, in 2007. Most of the barriers are economic, social, institutional and political. That is why the next set of IPCC reports will put a major focus on the solutions for reaching that zero-carbon society, hopefully helping to overcome those barriers by examining the options for action.

That said, there are significant gaps in our knowledge about the challenges and risks associated with some of the technologies that have been mentioned as contributing to a carbon-free economy. These include carbon dioxide removal, afforestation, and BECCS – the combination of bioenergy and CCS, where CO2 is absorbed from the atmosphere by growing biomatter such as trees, which are then burned in power plants while sequestering the resulting emissions.

We do not yet know enough about the extent to which these technologies can be scaled up, and hence what their potential is. Planting forests to absorb carbon or provide energy would eventually run up against the need for land for food.

Examining these questions will be another focus of our forthcoming reports. Without prejudging the scoping processes of the forthcoming reports, there are some important areas of research – many overlapping between science, technology and the social sciences – that we are likely to assess.

The decarbonisation of electricity generation will involve large-scale deployment of renewables, nuclear and CCS. What are the risks and opportunities here? What do we know about CCS – not only its operational safety, but also the risks of transporting sequestered CO_2 and the long-term integrity of storage?

The relationship between behavioural change and greater energy efficiency is fascinating. Climate change and cities, which are home to over half the world's population, is a growing area of research. Cities pose particular challenges to mitigation: as new cities are built and existing cities develop, how do planners avoid locking-in carbon-intensive infrastructure? And what are the prospects for sustainable transport, achieving zero-GHG mobility through renewables-based electricity or hydrogen?

Global Stocktake

How can the IPCC facilitate this search for solutions? Our next comprehensive assessment, the Sixth Assessment Report, will be completed in 2022, in time for the first global stocktake one year later. We are also updating the methodologies used by countries to measure and report their GHG emissions and removals.

And we are producing three special reports: on the impacts of global warming of 1.5°C above pre-industrial levels and related global GHG emissions pathways in the context of strengthening the global response to the threat of climate change, sustainable development and efforts to eradicate poverty; on climate change, desertification, land degradation, sustainable land management, food security and GHG fluxes interrestrial ecosystems; and on climate change and oceans and the cryosphere. The report on 1.5°C was specifically requested by COP21 and will be delivered in 2018.

All these reports will focus on the assessment of realistic response strategies in line with our mandate. We will strengthen our treatment of regional issues, as local and regional information is the most relevant for policymakers. We will improve the knowledge base for the interaction of climate change and cities, which will be one of the focuses of the Sixth Assessment Report. And the three special reports – requested by our member states and the UNFCCC – will address some of the most urgent and policy-relevant questions.

Hoesung Lee, Chair
Intergovernmental Panel on Climate Change[45]

Though the IPCC and the International Energy Agency recognize the challenges with carbon sequestration and storage, they still consider it "crucial for meeting emissions standards that can prevent the worst effects of climate change."[46] CSS has been criticized as expensive to build and a high-energy user. But we see from the *New York Times* that efforts like the Petra Nova carbon capture process are emerging as promising applications. Similar to how cogen and trigen recapture and reuse the excess heat generated; the Petra Nova process apparently reuses the CO_2 it captures from the coal-burning unit and then injects it into oil wells to increase oil recovery (a process called enhanced oil recovery).[47] It is expected to be operational around the same time this book is published.

THORIUM MOLTEN SALT REACTORS

For those concerned with the safety and efficacy of nuclear power plants, thorium is being seriously explored as a promising alternative fuel source for our energy-related challenges – climate change, energy needs and fluctuating availability of wind and solar power. Thorium is a radioactive chemical element designated as "Th" in the periodic table of elements.

One concept stage idea is Thorium-MOX, which combines thorium with uranium in a mix of thorium oxide and 10% uranium oxide for use in nuclear reactors. This thorium mix is being touted as a safer, more environmentally conscious alternative that is not as vulnerable to nuclear arms proliferation.[48]

Another type of thorium-based nuclear reactor, which we are focusing on here, is the Thorium Molten Salt Reactor (MSR). The Oak Ridge National Laboratory[49] in Tennessee first developed this concept. The earliest models were built in the U.S. during the 1960s – one of them operated from 1965 to 1969. India has embarked on a three-phase program with bullish objectives for construction; while the Czech Republic is active in research. But it seems China, in collaboration with Oak Ridge and others, may be on track to "build a small 2 to 10 megawatt research reactor."[50]

MSRs are far safer than conventional nuclear reactors that use solid fuel rods. MSRs use liquid fuel that neither overheat nor melt down. They have freeze plugs at their bottom that melt following an increase in heat inside the reactor and allow the liquid fuel salts to drain out into the emergency cooling tanks. In addition the reactive behavior of the fuel salt operates to regulate the nuclear reaction. While dropping temperatures cool the salt and intensify the nuclear reaction to generate heat and produce power; rising temperatures heat the salt up and slow down or even stop the nuclear reaction.

The Thorium Molten Salt Reactor[51]

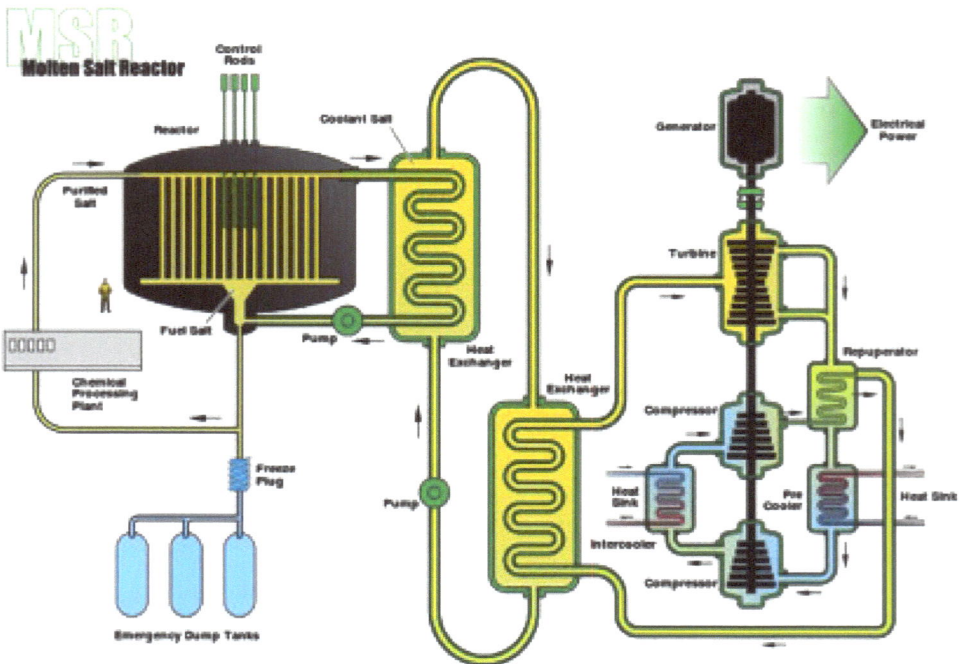

MSR
Molten Salt Reactor

Control Rods

Reactor

Coolant Salt

Generator

Electrical Power

Purified Salt

Fuel Salt

Pump

Heat Exchanger

Turbine

Recuperator

Chemical Processing Plant

Heat Exchanger

Compressor

Freeze Plug

Pump

Heat Sink

Pre Cooler

Heat Sink

Intercooler

Compressor

Emergency Dump Tanks

MSRs also do not pose the same long-term dangers of storing nuclear waste that occurs with conventional reactors. Typically, when the uranium inside the solid ceramic fuel rods splits (fissions) and releases certain gases, these ceramic rods then become susceptible to cracking. These ceramic rods must then be replaced even though they still contain un-used radioactive elements called actinides.[52] If not recycled, actinides in these quantities when buried remain radioactive for thousands of years. By contrast, the gases produced in MSRs by-pass to an off-gas unit, where they are cooled and removed. As a result, the liquid fuel is not affected by the gases and can remain in the reactor and continue to split until nearly all the actinides inside them are fully used. In these far reduced quantities, the remaining actinides are radioactive for only 300 or less years.[53]

Finally, because these actinides are nearly fully used, MSRs generate a tremendous amount of energy. To give you a sense of how efficient they are and how much energy they produce, consider: only 3.2 kilograms of fission fuel per day (a little less than eight pounds a day) is needed to fuel a MSR power plant that would provide 1,000 megawatts of electricity. Assuming one megawatt of electricity serves an average of 650 homes; 1,000 megawatts would provide enough electricity for 650,000 homes – from just eight pounds of thorium fuel salt.

Or, with just one gram (about one third of an ounce) of natural thorium, a MSR can produce the same amount of energy generated by 250 grams or 551 pounds of natural uranium (before enrichment) in light water reactors.

As a last example, 1,000 kg (2,204 pounds) of natural thorium in a MSR can produce enough electricity for one year for a city of one million. 7.3 million pounds of coal would be needed to produce this amount of energy!

The construction of MSRs and the technology they use also cost far less to build than conventional reactors given their simplified construction, fewer parts, less expensive safety systems, modular construction and simplified fuel and waste handling. They also "load follow" or back up the fluctuating supplies of wind and solar. MSRs do not need to ramp-up to generate electricity unlike gas plants, which use as much natural gas when ramping-up as being kept on all the time.[54]

GEOTHERMAL ENERGY

Geothermal technology harnesses the Earth's heat. Just a few feet below the surface, the Earth maintains a near-constant temperature, in contrast to the summer and winter extremes of the ambient air above ground. Farther below the surface, the temperature increases at an average rate of approximately 1°F for every 70 feet in depth. In some regions, tectonic and volcanic activity can bring higher temperatures and pockets of super-heated water and steam much closer to the surface. Three main types of technologies take advantage of Earth as a heat source: ground source heat pumps, direct use geothermal and deep enhanced geothermal systems. Geothermal energy is considered a renewable resource.

Ground source heat pumps and direct use geothermal technologies serve heating and cooling applications, while deep and enhanced geothermal technologies generally take advantage of a much deeper, higher temperature geothermal resource to generate electricity.

EPA[55]

The Dutch are using one such form of deep and enhanced geothermal system to provide geo-thermal heating and cooling called ATES (Aquifer Thermal Energy Storage).[56] In this process, they drill down about 100 meters (300 plus feet) to access the underground aquifer water. Their renewable energy technology uses the difference in temperature of surface water and the constant temperature of the underground aquifer water (of 57° F) to create energy.

During the summer, the surface water is warmer by 15° F than the aquifer water temperature; and during the winter the surface temperature is colder by 15° F than underwater. This temperature difference is used to create electrical energy, which is delivered through a ground source heat pump to thousands of buildings in the Netherlands. The government there has even created underground heat maps that monitor and distribute energy among the various buildings utilizing ATES.

Research is also showing that ATES can clean or "remediate polluted groundwater ten times faster than existing technologies."[57] As in a washing machine the "contaminated groundwater moves back and forth in the [ATES] underground tubes used for thermal storage" allowing micro-organisms to "eat the contamination attached to the contaminated soil particles."[58]

In the application of this technology to places like NYC and throughout the states of New York and New Jersey, an ideal set of conditions is needed to utilize ATES such as relatively easy to drill subsurface geology to reach water hundreds of feet underground. We also see, depending on what part of the country ATES is being considered, high electric costs in those areas may make this technology financially attractive as it in many parts of Europe.

A CLOSING ADMONITION

As some of these technologies are still being developed, tested and understood, James Lovelock suggests:

Until we know for certain how to cure global heating, our greatest efforts should go into adaptation, preparing those parts of the Earth least likely to be affected by adverse climate change as the safe havens for a civilized humanity. In choosing havens safe from serious climate change, we will need the guidance of the IPCC and perhaps they should be tasked to do this. More importantly, we have to stop pretending that there is any possible way back to that lush, comfortable, and beautiful Earth we left behind sometime in the twentieth century. The further we go along the path of business as usual, the more we are lost.

James Lovelock[59]

CHAPTER 9
THE MEEK INHERIT THE EARTH

The chasm between haves and have-nots in our society, in developed and developing countries, continues to grow. History teaches us that left unaddressed such chasms lead to violence as evidenced during the French Revolution and the two World Wars.

What is the advantage of relatively few people having vast resources at the expense of the many having too little? Should we be relying on non-representative monolithic financial institutions, global banks and corporations, or politicized bureaucracies to right the ship? Or should we all be playing our part? Should we be scaling up our collective approach in addressing climate change in ways that "champion small, appropriate technologies" and "empower the many rather than just the few."[60] What would a more just, inclusive business, economic and labor market look like? Are there any precedents out there?

SMALL IS BEAUTIFUL MODEL

One of the leading thinkers in this area was E.F. Schumacher. As a trained economist, he led the U.K. National Coal Board. The excerpt below provides a flavor of his thinking.

One of the most fateful errors of our age is the belief that 'the problem of production' has been solved. Not only is this belief firmly held by people remote from production and therefore professionally unacquainted with the facts – it is held by virtually all the experts, the captains of industry, the economic managers in the governments of the world, the academic and not-so-academic economists, not to mention the economic journalists. They may disagree on many things but they all agree that the problem of production has been solved; that mankind has at last come of age. For the rich countries, they say, the most important task now is 'education for leisure' and, for the poor countries . . . the 'transfer of technology' . . . .

[The] erroneous view that the "problem of production" has been solved . . . . so egregious and so firmly rooted [,] is closely connected with the philosophical, not to say religious, changes during the last three or four centuries in man's attitude to nature. I should perhaps say: western man's attitude to nature, but since the whole world is now in a process of westernization, the more generalized statement appears to be justified. Modern man does not experience himself as a part of nature but as an outside force destined to dominate and conquer it. He even talks of a battle with nature, forgetting that, if he won the battle, he would find himself on the losing side. Until quite recently, the battle seemed to go well enough to give him the illusion of unlimited powers, but not so well as to bring the possibility of total victory into view. This has now come into view, and many people, albeit only a minority, are beginning to realise what this means for the continued existence of humanity.

E.F. Schumacher[61]

Schumacher saw that man's relationship with nature and his environment had to be restored, and that people on the local level had to be engaged in the improvement of their lives. In an earlier article, published in *The Observer* in 1965, Schumacher criticized the transfer of large-scale technologies to developing countries that were not in the stage of development to utilize them. He argued instead that it would be more helpful if intermediate technologies were provided, ones that were in line with the needs and skills possessed by the people of developing countries.[62]

From this notion of "appropriateness" and "local needs" as guiding their interventions, he along with others including George McRobie, Julia Porter, Alfred Latham-Koenig and Mansur Hoda put this concept into practice. They created "advisory centres" to promote the use of efficient labor-intensive techniques, which led to the establishment of the Intermediate Technology Development Group (ITDG) in 1966. The ITDG increasingly became directly involved in local projects and successfully developed working groups in farming, energy, building materials and rural health.

Today, Practical Action, as it is now known, operates seven regional offices handling over 100 projects around the world.[63] Its mission is provided on the next page.

PROJECT WORK OF PRACTICAL ACTION[64]

Practical Action works in partnership with poor people and their communities, building on their own knowledge and skills to come up with innovative, sustainable and practical solutions. The organisation's project work is based around four international goals:

○ Energy access - sustainable access to modern energy services

○ Food and agriculture - sustainable systems of agriculture and natural resource management that provide food security and livelihoods for the poor

○ Urban water and waste - improved access to drinking water, sanitation and waste services for the poor

○ Disaster risk reduction - reduced risk of disasters for marginalized groups and communities

At some point soon if we have any hope as a species of surviving the full effects of climate disasters, we will have to decide if we are nasty and brutish as Sir Thomas Hobbes believed in his classic book, *The Leviathan,* deserving the end of our species; or whether we are deserving to be lifted by each other. In either case, the earth will adjust, as it has in for millennia, with or without us. Our book cover may appear to draw this cautionary note from *The Leviathan* by depicting grasping hands. But our hands move towards each other and within them they hold humanity.

Schumacher saw for us an economic framework that gives individuals a central role and situates production at a local site rather than farmed out to various distant locations for cost savings. Allowing individuals within the community to experience the satisfaction of producing things in their entirety, in ways that reduce the cost of transporting and using distant materials, allows for a more meaningful method of production. Localizing work also allows for workers to live closer to their homes, so they can spend more time with their families and participate in their communities, rather than having to travel or commute for long hours. For this reason, we support those cities that offer an ecosystem of employment opportunities, public transit, schools and a sustainable, resilient quality of life.

Eric's oldest friend, Michael Shuman, has been advocating localization of our economies and politics for over 30 years. He has written nine books on the subject! In *Local Dollars, Local Sense*, he argues for American investors to move their money from Wall Street to Main Street. Shuman points out that locally owned businesses comprise more than half the economy. They also generate profit rates that equal or exceed those of Fortune 500 companies. For over a decade, they have competed successfully to maintain their share of jobs and output (also called market share). And still, investors have systematically shunned them.

Consider, as he has, the potential impact of moving half of our financial capital into the local half of the economy on jobs, income and wealth. Currently there is about $50 trillion in stocks, bonds, mutual funds, pension funds and insurance funds. A portion of that invested in Main Street businesses would strengthen communities of all sizes and benefit a much broader spectrum of our society.

These thinkers and these precedents – past and current – provides us with some of the tools to start rebalancing our economy and business practices towards a Small is Beautiful model, one which places greater consideration on the role of the individual in the production of goods and services, and allows that individual to see and benefit from the fruits of such labor.

CHAPTER 10
WHAT IF WE DON'T GET OUR ACT TOGETHER?

Another coastal city, Miami. Source: Arlen Stawasz.

How bad is it? The short answer is that it is much worse than most people know and it will most probably get worse in the coming years and decades. What are the consequences?

Among the casualties of climate change are the decline of several species like the orange-spotted filefish totally dependent on coral reefs; polar bears being forced to find other food sources on land as the arctic sea ice retreats;[65] adélie penguins living on krill whose numbers are falling as their habitat under the Antarctic seas ice retreats; and North Atlantic cod whose ecosystem in the northeastern coast in North America has changed.[66] Then there are the reductions in the number of bees worldwide, whose role in our food supply is critical: "bees are responsible for one out of every three bites of food we eat."[67]

Global warming is adversely affecting the food producing areas of our country as in California. The other night as Eric was enjoying a mid-night snack of Maranatha Almond Butter made with California Almonds, it dawned on him that almond production may soon be a thing of the past because of the water crisis. The enormous demands of growing these types of food on decreasing supplies of water in a desert-like climate will force government officials and legislators to allocate the use of water among equally essential needs: water for drinking, water for growing food and water for producing energy. Leaders with the wisdom of King Solomon have to be ready to make such difficult decisions.

Fresh water is so important to our lives that it bears repeating: we need water for our sustenance, food production and energy production. It is not infinite in supply as evidenced in California's droughts and other desert environments. We must become more judicious in how we develop our communities given their effect on water consumption, for example, promoting sustainable communities within the desert (oases of sustainable living) over unsustainable forms of suburban sprawl.

Normally during winter, the Los Angeles River is replenished – not so this year. Source: Arlen Stawasz (2016)

A SHIP CALLED EARTH

> There are no mere passengers aboard United Spaceship Planet Earth. We are all crew.[68]
>
> Buckminster Fuller

This quote reminds us of the invisible boundaries that divide our countries and limit our ability to address the many social, economic and environmental stressors. These are boundaries that climate change does not recognize.

In "this ship," sadly, many perceive they are entitled to occupy certain sections, or only to do certain tasks. Some even believe they own parts of "this ship." Meanwhile, the ship's upkeep and maintenance have been sorely neglected. But we can learn what it will take to address and cope with the effects of flooding from the efforts being taken in The Netherlands and, by contrast, what is at stake in human lives being lost in Bangladesh.

NETHERLANDS: A SHIFT IN POLICY

This section comes from work done by our colleague Arlen Stawasz of the architectural firm, Perkins+Will. The Netherlands – a country slightly less than twice the size of New Jersey – has developed an expertise on how to live and work with water.

Much of the country falls into "low and flat lands in the west and north, and the higher lands with minor hills in the east and south."[69] Nearly half of the low and flat lands have an elevation of less than 1 meter or 3.3 feet above sea level, with much of the surface below sea level.[70]

In 1953, a major storm flooded the southern part of Holland, the Netherlands, and killed 1,863 people. This flood was considered the worst in Dutch history. It resulted in a coordinated, concerted and significant strengthening of coastal defenses. The Dutch spent billions of euros (where one euro is almost equal to one dollar) building a protective system called the Delta Works – a comprehensive system focused on "keeping the water out." With an annual 7 billion euro budget, this program employs over 20,000 individuals. Their operations span 4,000 pump stations and oversee close to 14,000 kilometers (8,699 miles) of dams and dikes.

They intended that their strategy of "keeping the water out" would resolve the many water threats that the Netherlands faces: increased precipitation, sea level rise, sinking land and saline intrusion into their crops and agriculture. Instead the Dutch have discovered this is a losing battle. The more they try to control the water, the more it controls them.

As a result they have shifted their approach to "making room for the river." Under this approach, the Dutch are incorporating into land ownership, the concept of giving the land back to nature and building the earth's natural systems.   A Dutchman once said, "it can take me 5 years of my life to build a bridge over the river, but it will take me the rest of my life, to keep the river underneath the bridge."

Today the Netherlands is developing a collective consciousness of learning to live with nature's water systems, and turning the negative threats and vulnerabilities into a productive economy built on its ecology. This is about giving back what they once thought was theirs.

The Netherlands. The Maeslantkering Storm Surge Barrier Delta Works
Source: Arlen Stawasz

BANGLADESH: WATER INUNDATION

By contrast, Bangladesh has lost many people to – and millions have been rendered homeless by – the damaging impact of its many water-related risks.

An image of some children displaced by climate change
in Dhaka, Bangladesh. Source: Arlen Stawasz

"Roughly 80% of the landmass is made up of fertile alluvial lowland"[71] called the Ganges-Brahmaputra Delta or Bengal Delta. Here most of its elevations are less than 10 meters or 33 feet above sea level. Filled with over 700 rivers that crisscross throughout the country, the Bengali Delta is considered the most delicate and diverse ecological system in the world. For this reason it is also known as the Green Delta. The rivers that flow from the Himalayan Alps are considered the country's bloodline. Yet, the increase of unmonitored factory and chemical pollution and contamination in the water systems are destroying these environments.

Bangladesh also faces cyclones, river flooding, monsoon rainfall, water logging, water contamination and the chronic stress associated with sea level rise. In 1970, the worst cyclone in Bengali history resulted in over 550,000 casualties. In 1991, the country had another cyclone hit the coast, which resulted in over 150,000 casualties with millions of dollars lost in destroyed land assets. In 2007, Cyclone Sidr hit the coast killing about 3,500 people. These storms are not only killing people and destroying properties; they are causing human migration and resettlements into some of the most densely populated cities on the planet like Dhaka.[72] This is one of the "ground zero" areas for climate change; and it is only getting worse.

Today, approximately 10 million people are homeless in Dhaka, the city capital of Bangladesh. Nearly 7 million of these homeless people have been displaced by climate related disasters. Some 25 million people are projected to be homeless in this country by 2025 – this only eight years from the publication year of this book! Almost 10-20% of villagers migrate away from the coast each year; while 50% of the population in Dhaka lives in slums. Living conditions are difficult with health and wellness being major issues. There also does not appear to be government solution for the refugees affected by climate change.

With the number of people being displaced by climate related disasters around the world on the rise, from far too much water or not enough, how many more lives do we have to lose before we can really learn to live with the planet, instead of working against it?

Image of the Bengali Delta. Source: Google Stock Photos

CHAPTER 11
PLAN RELOCATION / PLAN R

THE HUMAN CONDITION

We humans find it difficult to think beyond our lifetimes, which is why many cannot grasp the full disastrous impact of climate change on our way of life. With the personal difficulties each of us and our families face, we find it challenging to understand and empathize with situations other than our own – this includes different locations as well as different set of circumstances.

If we cannot marshal the collective will and collective action in this country and the world to put into effect Brown's Plan B – "Save the Civilization" through a green economy – we will need a contingency plan to protect our species. Our Plan Relocation is that alternative plan. Even if you do not believe in climate change, the existence of flood and drought zones on our planet will force millions of vulnerable people to relocate. We want to be ready with sustainable and resilient communities on "higher ground."

With the projected widespread increase in demands upon national governments to fund future disasters, municipalities and their residents should not assume that, in the future, such funds would be available. In fact, by one measure of future viability, the National Flood Insurance Program run by FEMA already owes the U.S. Treasury $23 billion.[73] This program had been intended to be self-funding through policyholder premiums, but the "catastrophic hurricanes Katrina in 2005 and Sandy in 2012 caused so much damage that the program could not pay for it all."[74] Instead after Katrina, Congress had to increase FEMA's borrowing authority from $2 billion to more than $20 billion and then, after Sandy, to $30 billion.[75]

By another measure, residential property taxes are insufficient to provide municipalities with a cushion needed to recover from the effects of extreme weather events. Such disasters only reduce and stress their revenues as businesses close down and tourism declines along with an increase in demand for public services like cleanup, homeless shelters, temporary housing, food pantries, clothing, medical supplies and emergency healthcare.

Municipalities will have to consider strategies to decrease their vulnerabilities by investing in resiliency and hardening infrastructure. They will likely also have to increase property taxes; reduce operation costs through a combination of decreased municipal services and out-sourcing; and even decide upon managed retreat from their coastal or drought-ridden areas.

But no one, no economist, public official or businessperson, can easily account for the difficult personal and emotional impact to the affected residents, some of whom have been living in these areas for generations. Still as difficult as these conversations and decisions will be, we must demand that our government officials exercise the leadership and have the courage and foresight to begin the necessary action now. We provide in Appendix E one approach to how policymakers can analyze the costs / benefits to climate resilience projects and better make capital budget decisions within this new environment.

MARKING TIME

Let's start with some of our pivotal dates, call them milestones for the future of the human race: 2020, 2035, 2050, 2080 and 2100.   You may also want to read Gwynne Dyer's take on future scenarios and what might occur in his book *Climate Wars*.

These dates are keyed to keeping global warming from increasing beyond an extra 2° C (about 3.6° F). In addition to this commitment, the 195 countries in the Paris Agreement would also work towards a reduced warming of 1.5° C (about 2.7° F).

Some experts like Scott Barrett of Columbia University, who served on the U.N.'s Climate Panel, believe the 2° C target was chosen "more for political reasons than for true scientific reasons. . . [so] countries could agree on a collective target, that that would mobilize the action needed to get the whole world to act together."[76] A warming of 2° C would result in longer droughts, more intense heat waves, big disruptions to the world food supply, sea level rising by several feet, flooding of many coastal communities in the U.S. and, potentially, large migrations of people from countries like Bangladesh, India and Vietnam.[77]

The second target, 1.5° C, in the Paris Agreement reads as an "aspirational" objective. But the inclusion of this second number, we think, reflects the belief by many scientists and climate experts that 2° C is not enough. The United Nations Framework Convention on Climate Change (UNFCCC) and others, instead, believe that 2° C should be established as "an upper limit, a defense line that needs to be stringently defended, while less warming would be preferable."[78] In addition, many like the International Energy Agency see that we have only a 50% chance of achieving this hard stop at 2° C. They reason why not increase the probability of reaching this objective by lowering the target to 1.5° C.[79]

To achieve these two targets with varying levels of probability or desire, the Oil Change International here prescribes the needed actions.[80] We've organized their milestones by year and have added some helpful commentary. You will see ambiguous phrases like "a high certainty," "medium chance" or "good chance" as all falling short of a guarantee. And all these dates occur not so distant in the future in the lifetimes of our Millennials and Post-Millennials.

NOW	For a **66% chance** of achieving the 2° C target or a **50% chance** of achieving the 1.5° C target "global emissions must peak and begin declining immediately." This requires adopting a policy of carbon neutrality or a net zero carbon footprint.
2026	A **high certainty** of avoiding a warming of 1.5 ° C requires net zero carbon footprint.
2050	A **medium chance** to avoid a warming of 1.5 ° C requires net zero carbon footprint.
2065	A **good chance** of avoiding a warming of 2 ° C requires net zero carbon footprint.

With this in mind, we see the following as important years.

2020	The year that the Paris Agreement / COP21 has developed countries transfer $100 billion annually to developing countries for climate adaptation. The target date under Brown's Plan B for reducing 80% of carbon emissions to keep the rise of CO_2 from reaching 400 ppm in 2020 – except we are already currently at 400 ppm.
2035	Based on current 400 ppm, if we are not successful in Brown's Plan B, we will be at 450 ppm, at which point we only have a 50% chance of avoiding catastrophic global warming where average global temperature rises beyond 2° C.[81]
2050	Projected human population reaches 9 billion. The sea level rise is expected to increase exponentially after this year especially if ppms are not stabilized or reduced. Under current plans, majority of world is trying to reduce 80% of our current carbon emissions by this year. Food, water and energy supply issues may be a top priority.
2080	How exactly climate feedbacks influence sea level rise remains to be seen but they can very well cause SLR to accelerate exponentially in the years that follow 2050. If so, human misery will be rampant by this time. Human migration will likely become a national and global priority.

| 2100 | This new century will likely present a very different world than we know today. Should the projected events follow the timetable and trajectory of global warming that sea level experts predict, by the 22nd century Plan Relocations of the type we propose will be required – but on a massive scale. At the same time, more definite explorations of other planets for possible migrations may also be needed. |

AREAS VULNERABLE TO CLIMATE CHANGE

Standard & Poor's identified five countries and their economies as being most vulnerable to the effects of climate change. In particular they looked at the role that agriculture plays in the country's gross domestic product and the vulnerability index as developed by the Notre Dame University Global Adaptation Index (Notre Dame Adaptation Index). These five countries are Cambodia, Vietnam, Bangladesh, Senegal and Mozambique.[82]

From this Notre Dame Adaptation Index, the majority of Africa and South Asia including China are considered the most vulnerable and least ready to handle climate change.[83] Their vulnerability stems from the "potential impact of climate change on [their] food, water, health, ecosystem service, human habitat and infrastructure."[84]

Most of the developed countries are less vulnerable and better prepared to cope with the impact of climate challenge. Still some cities within Europe, Canada, the U.S. and Latin America are vulnerable to "sea-level rise, extreme precipitation and drought, urban heat islands and changes to average temperature and precipitation." These vulnerable areas include Cartagena, London and Rotterdam – though considerable measures are being taken in some of these areas to increase their resiliency.

Within the U.S., the top 10 cities by order of being most vulnerable are: New Orleans, Minneapolis, Las Vegas, the coastal areas of Lower Manhattan and Brooklyn, Kansas City, Boston, Denver, St Paul, Washington D.C. and Philadelphia.[85] And while Miami is widely reported as being the most vulnerable, it is ranked as being the 19th most vulnerable U.S. city given other factors considered by experts at The Weather Channel. Still some scientists believe Miami's "layers of limestone, porous rock that doesn't prevent water from infiltrating," and the "flooding there could eventually make much of the city unlivable."[86]

Many scientific studies indicate that the area between the Tropic of Capricorn at the southern hemisphere to the Tropic of Cancer, its northern counterpart, will become a desert. This process will trigger, we believe, a human migration from south to north that constitutes The Great Climate Diaspora at some point soon.

In the long run, when factoring in sea level rise, many experts calculate nearly 40% of the world population will be affected. To put this in perspective, India and China account for nearly 40% of the world population and their coastal areas are extremely vulnerable to sea level rise.[87]

The Julia Tuttle Causeway leading to Miami Beach surrounded by water. Source: Arlen Stawasz

WHERE TO MOVE PEOPLE

Future decisions as to <u>where</u> people should be relocated, or <u>in which</u> cities and communities to invest and further develop as relocation areas should start with a consideration of their future sea level rise (SLR). The amount of SLR can range anywhere from 1 foot to 6 feet by year 2100 according to most scientist predictions. Where in this range the sea level rises will depend on how fast the polar ice caps melt.

If and as the polar ice caps melt quicker than estimated, positive feedbacks or secondary actions can accelerate the melting with the effect of increasing the amount of SLR. For example, the world's largest peat bog – a massive region of permafrost peat bog formed 11,000 years ago at the end of the last ice age – in Western Siberia is melting. As its permafrost melts it causes a positive feedback of releasing, over decades, large quantities of methane – a heat trapping, greenhouse gas.

These positive feedbacks can become tipping points where "a small change can have large, long-term consequences for a system." Timothy Lenton lists such various positive feedbacks as permafrost melting and collapse; increasing absorption of solar radiation that is heating and melting the bottom of the sea ice; atmospheric circulation bringing warm air and warm ocean currents from the Atlantic into the Arctic; continued melting at the margins of the Greenland Ice Sheet; and warming ocean waters and longer snow-free seasons.[88] How these feedback relationships trigger and accelerate climate change and the melting of the polar ice caps and ice sheets is complicated. But the takeaway here is that increased warming at the poles and accelerated melting of the polar ice caps will likely cause the SLR to be massive – up to 200 feet by some scientific estimates – as the Antarctic sea ice significantly melts.

We have begun evaluating the ability of locations like Austin, Atlanta, Ashland and Asheville in the United States to accommodate increasing populations. Many other locations throughout different areas of the country and the world should be identified to plan for The Great Climate Diaspora. The NRF has developed and is using the following criteria as a threshold initial analysis for identifying ideal locations to relocate populations.

Criteria for Ideal Relocation Sites
The Natural Resilience Foundation

Elevation
Seek sites at an elevation of 100 meters or about 330 feet above sea level. <u>See Appendix C</u> that provides elevations of U.S. cities.

Water
Seeks sites where clean and fresh water is available.

Air
Seek sites where clean air exists.

Food
Seek sites where food can be locally grown.

Energy
Seek sites where energy can be generated or harnessed without reliance on a centralized grid.

Mass Transit
Seek sites where there exist opportunities for sustainable development, namely an existing mass or public transit infrastructure, as well as possible infrastructure for mass use of electric cars.[89]

Flat Land
Sites with plateau-like land able to accommodate multi-million people settlements.

Receptive Governance

> An accommodating, receptive socio, economic and political environment that allows the municipality to act quickly and decisively.

Conscious and Aware

> A socio, economic and political environment that when carrying out the establishment of these relocation cities and communities will, for example, utilize the principles of triple bottom line accounting to factor in the financial, social and the environmental impact of all technologies, building materials and development decisions.

RETREATS AND MOVEMENTS

Some cities and communities exist in low-lying elevations where they are at, close to or below sea level; other areas suffer from constant flooding; and still others have their coastal borders of land being claimed by the sea due to coastal erosion. In these situations, managed retreat (also known as managed realignment) requires such populations to leave, remove whatever coastal barriers or protections exist to allow the sea to reclaim these areas. There are also areas – as in Canada, Siberia and the Nordic countries – where land once under huge ice sheets is rebounding or rising in a process called isostatic rebound. Here managed retreat may also be necessary.

Leading thinkers and scientists like Klaus Jacob of Columbia's Lamont-Doherty Earth Observatory speak of "nomadic infrastructure" and other innovative methods to accommodate changing weather patterns in developing (and perhaps even developed) countries. Jacob's nomadic infrastructure could be moved as sea level rise encroaches on their current terra firma. A landscape architect who teaches at the University of Pennsylvania, David Gouverneur, speaks of informal settlements through what he terms as "landscape armatures." For some time now, the Dutch as well have incorporated movement through floating foundations[90] in their arsenal of strategies.

These concepts represent an evolution in the way we define how we live and what constitutes community, in ways that are flexible and adaptable to the environment.

In The Great Climate Diaspora, the general migration is going to be from southern regions northward: from Latin American countries to the U.S. and Canada, and African and Middle Eastern nations to Europe. As a result, it is conceivable that areas like Greenland will become habitable, even resilient in the face of the climate change.

NEW FRONTIERS: GREENLAND AND FRESH WATER HARVESTING

You should know that in Greenland, there is an independence movement from Denmark, the country that currently "owns" Greenland. Greenlanders also hope that oil drilling will provide them with the necessary financial resources to become and remain independent from Denmark.

With "water" becoming the new "oil," what if, instead of drilling for oil, Greenland harnesses the fresh water released from its melting glaciers and ships it to drought areas like California and other southern locales?

Could we apply the same level of energy, creative thinking and tremendous resources that we use to extract and transport fossil fuels to instead transport fresh water over large distances? Can we access the technological and transport methodologies to meet the growing (increasingly desperate) demand in drought areas with the fresh water that will be displaced when the ice melts as well as unlocked from the melting ice?

Experts project that fresh water will soon become the most precious commodity on our planet. Intense competition for fresh water will be driven by three sectors: energy, agriculture, and humans and animals for sustenance. Given the essential nature of water to our lives, managing it under free-market principles and market competition may not result in the most efficient or fair allocation. Motivated by profit, institutional, corporate and private investors will likely buy up fresh water sources and sell it to the highest bidder.

It is conceivable that water for growing vineyards and almonds may even win over the water drinking needs of the poor, when it pays more to cultivate vineyards and almond fields. Increasingly water will be treated as a commodity, traded over the stock market and become subject to speculation, water-banking and derivative trading.

CHAPTER 12
EPPS SYNDROME AND ITS ANTIDOTE

As we develop climate resilience, we must be willing to engage and understand those who exhibit what we call the EPPS Syndrome – a set of symptoms displayed by certain people when discussing climate change. You can diagnose the EPPS Syndrome when someone (1) refuses to discuss the potential ramifications of climate change, (2) refuses to understand climate change, (3) holds on to pre-conceived notions even when facts say otherwise, or (4) parrots statements by media figures.

Perhaps the EPPS Syndrome arises from a deep emotional attachment to where the individual lives, and discussing climate change raises the painful possibility of having to relocate in the event of a major disaster.

In this way, our <u>current</u> perspectives toward our **e**conomy, **p**olitics, **p**sychology and **s**ociology may be limiting our capacity to cope with the large-scale dislocations that extreme weather events will bring. We believe, however, a shift in these perspectives – an EPPS Shift – can give us the opportunity to structure our future communities into equitable, sustainable and resilient ones. So, what kinds of shifts along these various dimensions should we consider?

ECONOMIC ASPECTS

As the United Nations has rightfully pointed out in numerous occasions, there is no reason that any of our world population should be living in poverty.

The underlying reason, among other factors, for existing poverty is an inefficient allocation of resources, which can occur in market and mixed-market economies. Joaquin sees food, clean water and clean air as well as services such as education, skill development and healthcare as being so essential and fundamental to life and societal participation that they should be considered as "essentials."

One shift in this economic framework would be to identify what constitutes an "essential" where its provision is so vital for a fair and dignified standard of living and necessary for a stable society. The challenge would be to fashion a system that gives individuals access to such essentials while ensuring that providers and suppliers are compensated.

A second shift would be to utilize this essential-based framework in negotiating collective arrangements between developed and developing countries. Developed countries could agree to transfer such essentials to developing ones, where in exchange developing nations would limit their populations to stem overpopulation in areas that simply cannot support such numbers. The economic justification for having many children in poor countries, which once had its rationale in an agrarian, agriculture economy, has given way to more urbanized societies with their production methods now mechanized. And in many areas, climate change is further constraining food supplies.

In a recent update from the *New York Times*, the droughts in "Lesotho, Malawi, Mozambique, Swaziland, Zambia and Zimbabwe"[91] were brought on by an "extremely warm El Nino event, which came on top of a larger drying trend in the last few decades in parts of Africa."[92] The result: families "slowly starving because rains and crops have failed for the last few years" and "reduced to eating cactus and even rock or ashes."[93]

A third shift in our economic systems would be to factor in the "true cost" of all goods, services and commodities through triple bottom line accounting. In this way the costs of production, manufacturing and transport on the environment as well as the costs of utilizing raw materials and natural resources as water, air, food, precious metals would be reflected.

A fourth shift is a consideration of universal income or universal jobs as a bridge between our current monetary-based world economy and a more resource-oriented society. Universal income or universal jobs can also be utilized in instances of massive dislocation and to "seed" the establishment of new communities. In such scenarios, displaced and relocated individuals would receive a sufficient income with which to start their lives. Such a framework can incorporate the need for basic income and the opportunity to undertake entrepreneurial endeavors and take on additional employment.

The *New York Times* reported that the Finnish Government is piloting a program of universal income to address, in part, the impact of thousands of skilled engineers laid off by Nokia. In this pilot program, the government will be considering the following issues.

"Will more people pursue jobs or start businesses? How many will stop working and squander their money on vodka? Will those liberated from the time-sucking entanglements of the unemployment system use their freedom to gain education, setting themselves up for promising new careers? These areas of inquiry extend beyond economic policy, into the realm of human nature."[94]

We believe in the face of climate disaster threatening multi-millions of people, the little that will be asked of everyone is worth saving humans as a species. Or put another way, even if more than a little is asked of everyone, it should be worth it to protect and preserve life. But where our existing systems appear to serve a mere few, we need to summon the courage to ask the difficult questions, and collectively as a people decide what really matters to us. Then with the will to act, aided by innovation, technology and creativity, this EPPS Shift can occur.

POLITICAL ASPECTS

The first time a hard decision of undertaking managed retreat or relocating affected populations comes, as in the refortification of New Orleans in the aftermath of Hurricane Katrina, such a possibility is generally not raised, or like the "elephant in the room" is avoided. New Orleans post-Katrina illustrates the competing social, economic and political concerns where an expedient (even if ultimately more financially expensive) solution wins over long-term sustainable or resilient alternatives.

The average elevation of New Orleans is between 1-2 feet below sea level, with some areas only being as high as 20 feet above sea level as at the base of the river levee in Uptown. Other areas lie as low as 7 feet <u>below</u> sea level as in the farthest reaches of Eastern New Orleans.[95] More starkly, "70 percent of its population" lives in a floodplain.[96]

The Army Corps of Engineers spent "$14.5 billion on fortifications to protect some 900,000 people living in the toe-tip of Louisiana"[97] – that figure was as of August 18, 2015. Admittedly, "the ring of protection around New Orleans is a vast improvement over the old system of federal levees and flood walls that failed catastrophically during Katrina."[98] But the Corps refers to this ring of protection as a "risk reduction system," as they "didn't want the public to be deluded into thinking that they were protected, that they're safe, that once we have a system that was complete they were relieved from any risk of flooding."[99]

How homes in the southern tip of Louisiana, unprotected by levees, are often built on stilts or elevated. Source: Arlen Stawasz

So, another opportunity came to revisit the wisdom of managed retreat and relocation. It came in a different area when Superstorm Sandy devastated the Rockaways in New York City and a very thin strip of land surrounded by the Jamaica Wildlife Preserve. Governor Andrew Cuomo offered "to spend as much as $400 million to purchase homes wrecked by Superstorm Sandy, have them demolished and then preserve the flood-prone land permanently, as undeveloped coastline."[100]

Portion of the levee prior to Katrina, about 20 feet high.
Source: Arlen Stawasz

Ultimately, most homeowners preferred to stay in the area and build back their homes. Continuing to press the point of buy-outs for a managed retreat remained too much of a "hot potato" especially for residents who simply love the Rockaways. Such love cannot prevent that at some point in the future this entire area will be reclaimed by nature and simply become part of the Jamaica Bay wildlife preservation area.

Post-Katrina, elevated homes in New Orleans. Source: Arlen Stawasz

PSYCHOLOGICAL ASPECTS

Quite justifiably the notion of having to relocate, surrendering to managed retreat proved to be just too traumatizing as we saw in Princeville and the Rockaways. But like it or not the necessity of relocating will present itself somewhere in this country and many parts of the world at some point soon. By then many will not have the luxury of a choice or avoiding the psychological trauma.

The Dutch have much to share on this topic and perhaps we can learn from them. They have been relocating people out of flood situations as most of their land is situated below sea level. In fact, it is Dutch government policy that every citizen be afforded the cost of relocation. Those who remain in the area will be living without government support and services once that area is deemed a stranded asset. The Dutch have learned that some things are better off not litigating and fighting over; and once they have made a decision over areas being flooded or underwater, they adhere to that decision and move forward.

SOCIOLOGICAL ASPECTS

After the managed retreat and relocation effort, we must contend with the question: How will those being relocated interact as a society? This is no small concern as the numbers of people being forced to relocate because of extreme weather events may number in the millions and tens of millions.

Consider the numbers of people already living in many coastal cities around the world and, even, in the U.S. Al Gore recognized a "double displacement" of people is occurring: first their displacement from rural areas to coastal cities and, second, from those same coastal cities to some other place. We see as a

variation of the second displacement, a third potential displacement is in store when cities re-develop areas and current
inhabitants must move to another place within that city or
state.

A second concern of sociological importance is what kind of
communities do we create? At what scale should these communities exist? Do we simply create new monolithic high-rise
cities out of flood and drought zones, or in new relocation
sites? Well-regarded architect, Vishaan Chakrabarty sees the
value in hyper-densification of cities with public transit infrastructure as being ideal sites for promoting sustainable living.
In *Country of Cities*,[101] he maintains that the more density of
people housed in a city with public transit, the less dependency
on automobiles and the greater the opportunities for sustainable practices. Indeed, evidence clearly indicates that single- and
low-density housing units consume far more energy than do
high-rise and attached buildings. There is also, Chakrabarty
adds, the virtue of affordable housing where the costs of constructing each unit of housing decrease as you increase the
number of floors in a building.

As urban planners and architects debate over whether to go the
way of hyper-density cities as advised by Chakrabarty, or build
communities on a livable scale, the sheer numbers of people
displaced or forced to relocate from coastal cities and low-lying
areas as well as drought-stricken locations will require some
level of high density developments. And some of these cities
will have to be very dense, high-rise cities, indeed.

Only time will tell how people will respond to The Great Climate Diaspora. Will inhabitants of vulnerable areas like New
Orleans, Miami and Cartagena, to name a few, stand their
ground (so to speak) and not move, or will the threat of perish-

ing overcome their desire to stay and fear of relocating? At that time, will our legislators and leaders be ready to act?

CHAPTER 13
FROM STRANDED ASSETS TO OPPORTUNITIES

A stranded asset is one that is no longer viable due to changing economic, social or environmental conditions. Examples are locations that do not have enough water or too much water. If the inability to produce food and the lack of water become major issues a place can become a stranded asset with literally no future value.

A variation on the concept of stranded assets would be "failed states," which as Brown points out largely exist on the life support provided by the international community. This support is given to these failed states so as to not to have to relocate the people living there to other points around the globe.

Fossil fuels can also become stranded assets if, as a result of the shift from fossil fuel to natural, renewable sources, demand for them decreases. According to Gore, companies hold as much as $21 trillion of assets in fossil fuels.[102] Consider the effect of companies who own fossil fuels now having to write down or reduce the value of such stranded assets. The *New York Times* reported that more than $5 trillion dollars held in fossil fuels will be divested "as the global call for a clean energy economy continues to strengthen [with] a former top Mobil Oil executive and thousands of signatories join[ing] the DivestInvest Movement."[103] The "stunning number" of pledged disinvestment commitments highlights the "potential for the industry to be faced with reserves of fuels that cannot be burned if the targets are to be met – a prospect known as "stranded assets."[104]

Legislators and policymakers should also be considering the impact on the many individuals whose retirement and pension plans have stock in such assets. There will be a big need to soften the blow that the potentially substantial reductions in asset values inflict on companies and on ordinary people.

OPPORTUNITIES

Are there any opportunities when assets become stranded assets? Yes, it depends. You should not rebuild in an area that is stranded or will be stranded as it lies in low-lying elevations, at or below sea level. You will only be throwing good money after bad. Over time, sea level rise and extreme weather events will only make these areas ever more vulnerable.

Our investments in the community, in real estate, in asset regeneration must take the long-view over short-term profit. Under this long-term view, where large swaths of coastal areas may be lost to coastal erosion and rising sea levels, planning and development efforts today must account for that future even if for now those locations are not stranded assets.

Following this long-term view, in certain areas in danger of becoming, for example, a water park or conversely a desert, there may be opportunities to still rebuild new, sustainable and resili-

ent communities <u>provided</u> the adequate types of resilient infrastructure are constructed. But in other instances, nature's trajectory cannot be managed and retreat is the recommended
strategy with existing communities being relocated elsewhere.

The real opportunity in real estate development is forward
thinking, understanding the trajectory of climate change and
identifying locations throughout the country that possess resilient characteristics. Then we would leverage these characteristics by constructing relocation communities that can
accommodate those displaced by extreme weather events.
Shifting real estate portfolios away from already vulnerable
coastal areas or drought-stricken sections is the best way to
avoid being left behind holding a portfolio of stranded assets.

Opportunities clearly exist as fossil fuels face the danger of becoming stranded assets. The logical corporate decision would
be to embrace renewable energy, deploy capital to acquire
promising renewable energy companies, and participate in the
transition from fossil fuel-based economies to renewable energy economies. Companies and investors who re-deploy their
capital will create real new growth, new job opportunities as
well as enjoy the positive perception as responsible stakeholders.

According to "The Climate Accountability Scorecard," provided by the Union of Concerned Scientists that rank major fossil
fuel companies on climate deception, disclosure and action[105]
none of these companies "has made a clean break from disin-
formation on climate science and policy."[106] Still along various
metrics relative to this group of fossil fuel companies, there
appear some bright spots: British Petroleum (BP) and Shell
publicly support COP21 / Paris Agreement and its goal of limiting emissions; BP and ConocoPhillips (Conoco) support fair
and effective climate policies; and Conoco and Exxon

acknowledge that climate change is contributing to the physical risks faced by their business.[107]

More telling is how investors in light of the declining "cost of wind, solar and electric cars" are predicted to be re-doubling their investments in wind, solar and other alternative sources of power.[108] The following are excerpts taken from a recent reporting by the *New York Times* on this important opportunity.[109]

> Clean energy companies will continue to thrive during a Trump administration, regardless of what the president says or does. The sector has become as much about getting returns on investments and catching the next technological boom as it is about reducing greenhouse gases and helping the environment.
>
> And clean energy is creating jobs in every state, not just the ones that have oil or gas in the ground. Even the most politically conservative states, like Kansas and Iowa, are leaders in wind power and are likely to continue investing in it.
>
> "No longer is there a trade-off between what you believe in and what you can make money off of," said Nancy Pfund, a founder and managing partner of DBL Partners, which made early investments in Solar City and Tesla . . .
>
> She predicts that investors "are going to redouble their efforts to migrate their portfolios to a 21st-centry energy economy." Even without subsidies… alternative energy sources will be well positioned to compete with coal and other carbon spewers.

The coal industry still appears to be lagging but we see an opportunity for this industry to embrace renewable energy technologies and deploy and invest in them in areas where they are currently located. In this way coal companies can redevelop former and existing coal-mining communities within West Virginia, Pennsylvania and parts of upstate New York.

Companies that see the opportunities that change can bring in the transition to a fossil-free economy will be the companies that survive. Many of these companies already have substantial capital reserves, access to technology, real estate holding and other valuable resources – but to protect these from being stranded they must begin the transition now. Those companies that fight to hold on to obsolete industries and technologies will eventually perish but not before they waste a lot of time and money.

The NRF's concept of Plan Relocation – the establishment of new, the expansion of existing and the retrofitting, repurposing of existing communities and cities into sustainable and resilient locations – is a plan for saving multi-millions faced with dislocation and unlocking the unbounded opportunities that come from rebuilding our economies and our communities.

PLANNING FOR RELOCATION COMMUNITIES AND CITIES

At The NRF we conceptualized how we would utilize $100,000,000 for the planning of sustainable and resilient communities or cities. The development of our plan will be guided by the criteria first presented in Chapter 11 and provided again on the following page.

Criteria for Ideal Relocation Sites
The Natural Resilience Foundation

Elevation   Seek sites at an elevation of 100 meters or about 330 feet above sea level. <u>See Appendix C</u> that provides elevations of U.S. cities

Water   Seeks sites where clean and fresh water is available.

Air   Seek sites where clean air exists.

Food   Seek sites where food can be locally grown.

Energy   Seek sites where energy can be generated or harnessed without reliance on a centralized grid.

Mass Transit   Seek sites where there exist opportunities for sustainable development, namely an existing mass or public transit infrastructure, as well as possible infrastructure for mass use of electric cars.

Flat Land   Sites with plateau-like land able to accommodate multi-million people settlements.

Receptive Governance

An accommodating, receptive socio, economic and political environment that enables the prospective municipality to act quickly and decisively.

Conscious and Aware

A socio, economic and political environment that when carrying out the establishment of these relocation cities and communities will, for example, utilize the principles of triple bottom line accounting to factor in the financial, social and the environmental impact of all technologies, building materials and development decisions.

On the following page we provide a roadmap for the planning activities we would undertake with a $100 million planning fund. Keep in mind that initiatives of this scale, as we show in our Powerpoint deck in Appendix G, require extensive design, planning, environmental investigation, cleanup and approvals. We believe 10 years will be needed for this endeavor and, if construction occurs within the following 10 years, the first round of relocation communities could be completed by 2040. This timetable does allow for an additional ten years that would bring us to 2050 as the latest build-out date.

$100,000,000 Planning Fund
The Natural Resilience Foundation

1   **Identify Suitable Site Locations**. Based on the criteria provided above, with special attention to "elevation, elevation, elevation" as the new real estate mantra, select 10 sites around the U.S. Sites would include the Northwest area of the country, like the Dakotas, Montana and the Great Lakes region. See Appendix C that provides elevations of U.S. cities.

Three sites would be existing cities suitable to be a relocation city. These locations would be appropriate for a range of small-sized communities housing an initial population of 50,000 to 250,000 people with the potential to grow tenfold in the future from 500,000 to 2.5 million. There would be also cities starting at 500,000 people with an expanded target of 5 million people in the future. One site will be planned as a megalopolis to support an eventual population of 25 million people.

For existing cities, we have been considering, for example, Asheville in North Carolina, Austin in Texas and Atlanta in Georgia. Former mining towns in California, Nevada, West Virginia, Pennsylvania and other areas of the country will also be evaluated, perhaps to re-create new versions of "Company Towns" or "Re-Settlements" of varying scale depending on the site and resources.

2   **Design a Sustainable and Resilient Community.** Within these varying small- to larger-sized communities as well as cities and megalopolis, design must address how best to spatially and physically organize, orient and layout these communities into smaller, more livable scales.

Cohesiveness, collaboration, creativity, entrepreneurship and sense of place are the governing principles we believe will promote social and economic sustainability; and these may be better achieved within smaller self-contained communities. During this early concept stage, we would bring community focus groups drawn from the intended affected populations and affected locations. Having these smaller scales of population should allow for self-sustained infrastructure like district energy, mass transit, net zero carbon use, local food sourcing, telecommunications and Internet.

3   **Develop a Master Plan for 10 communities**. These master plans will either call for expansion of existing communities or cities, the establishment of new ones, or the retrofitting of existing ones.

4   **Develop Appropriate Political and Governance Structures**. Explore and re-think how the benefits of some bureaucracy and systematization can be balanced with promoting creativity, entrepreneurship and small business. Utilizing digital technology platforms, we can be more efficient in managing resources and promoting shared resources, while also being more transparent and fair in how resources are distributed. Decision-making should shift the current reliance on profit and short-term results to one that is community focused and directed at constructing healthy, sustainable and resilient ecosystems.

5   **Rethink our Financial Structures**. The Great Recession of 2008 with all its multiple distortions demonstrated that our financial systems suffer from considerable levels of speculation, gaming, shifting risk, risk-taking and unaccountability.

Triple bottom line accounting should apply to all companies, public, private and not-for-profit, so as to reflect the true costs of their activities on the environment and promote responsible business operations and consumer practices.

6   **Secure Build-out Capital and Financing.** Utilize some portion of the $100 million to then raise private capital to build out the infrastructure along with public money. We would structure the appropriate public, private and community partnerships (PuPCos) for the sharing and flow of financial, intellectual property, development and community resources.

CHAPTER 14
The Great Climate Diaspora

At the core of this book and the enormous expected impact of climate change that we face as a species is the question of how to deal with a modern-day Global Diaspora. The Animal Kingdom already is relocating to different areas – troubled less, as it seems, by thinking too much. We, humans, need less thought and more action. We need to activate the more primordial side of our intellect by migrating to areas that are safer than the coastal cities that face increasing sea level rise.

IMMIGRATION CHALLENGES

Many experts predict migrants will escape the effects of extreme weather in their countries, as in the Middle East region like Syria and Yemen, by seeking entry into Europe. Short-term migration for these reasons is already starting to threaten national security within the European community. Some would even argue that one of the reasons the United Kingdom executed their Brexit strategy was to largely circumvent the migration that other European nations are facing.

Dyer, in his book, *Climate Wars*, conjectures that the U.K. will be favorably affected by future climate change as he believes their temperature and sea level rises will be modest. Still London is facing similar problems to those of New York City, with the flooding of the Upper Thames River. It is not clear whether some of the engineering solutions being discussed there will work, or accelerate the flooding where the linearity of such solutions may not capture or anticipate the complex set of reactions and interactions.

Medium-term immigration issues developing up until 2050 will most probably be even more formidable with many people suffering from a lack of food and water in much of the southern hemisphere. The combination of sea level rise with mass migrations northward will put enormous pressure on northern economies and will strain those countries into which people are immigrating and their attendant healthcare, financial and education systems. This speaks nothing about the cultural differences between residents and migrants arising from divergent religious, societal mores and ideologies. Equally disturbing will be nativist, nationalist and even isolationist attitudes that have been on the rise in recent years – attitudes that may well lead to wars.

The long-run immigration situation depends a lot on what we learn and what actually occurs between now and 2050. If sea level rise is projected to increase more rapidly starting in the mid-2040's it would seem we have about thirty years from now to get our house in order. From the perspective of Plan Relocation and the design of sustainable and resilient relocation communities and cities, we will need to be ready by 2050. So indeed, it would appear that as Hawking indicates, the next one hundred years are going to be very crucial in helping to save our species.

A WARNING ON THREAT MULTIPLIERS

If we continue our present course – of growing populations, short-term thinking, depleting natural resources, expanding coastal cities and continued rate of fossil-based energy consumption – threat multipliers over the scarcity of water, food and shelter essentials will only increase. Local, national and global stresses will stem from the populations seeking to relocate and emigrate from their own developing climate-affected countries. The countries where they go will also experience similar dislocations. We can expect increasing anxiety and increasing conflict and border wars.

The projected population growth figures in developing countries like Bangladesh, Indonesia, Philippines, India and Nigeria simply are not sustainable by any means. Unmitigated population growth is occurring in the very countries most vulnerable to flooding and drought. Providing essentials needed in these countries while also limiting population growth will be critical. As Brown points in Plan B "Save the Civilization," education of women (and men) about birth control and sexually transmitted diseases will be necessary.

CHAPTER 15
CASE STUDY: AUSTIN, TEXAS

One day in mid-2016, Eric, apparently along with another 139 people that day, decided to relocate to Austin, Texas. It seems like every twenty-five years or so, he gets wanderlust and must leave the New York area. His mother, whom he cares for part time, hates cold weather so she wanted a warm climate location in the United States. After looking at various cities along the east coast including Raleigh in North Carolina, Savannah in Georgia, and Naples in Florida, he decided on the only city that was west of the Mississippi: Austin, Texas.

View of Austin Skyline with Lakebird Lake at the foreground.
Source: Eric Kaufman (December 2016).

140 PEOPLE MOVE HERE DAILY

An average of 140 people moved to Austin each day during 2015; while in prior years the daily average was lower at 110 people. People mostly come from other parts of Texas and California. This daily relocation, of 51,000 new residents every year, adds to the existing Austin metropolitan population of 2 million. By 2050, assuming these numbers hold, the Austin metropolitan will grow to 3.7 million.

But this growth is nothing compared to what's happening in Dhaka, Bangladesh. This city grows by 500,000 inhabitants per year, or about 1,370 per day. Assuming stable growth, Dhaka will have 17 million more people by 2050.

Which of these cities can maintain this type of growth, given the flooding issues in Dhaka and the lack of water in Austin? We are finding that it is at the intersection of sustainability and resilience, where in the near future, cities that are sustainable and resilient will survive. For cities to survive and bounce back from future shocks like weather events and the possible short-ages in food, water and energy, they must have resilient and hardened infrastructure and redundant systems that ensure a ready supply of essential services and food and water. Sustain-able and resilient cities will be Darwin's "fittest" cities during the era of climate change.

As you can see on the following page, Austin tops the list of annual population growth among large U.S. cities by having an annual growth of 2.9%.

How fast did big cities grow last year?

Percent growth in the 50 largest U.S. cities, July 1, 2013 to July 1, 2014.
Source: U.S. Census Bureau

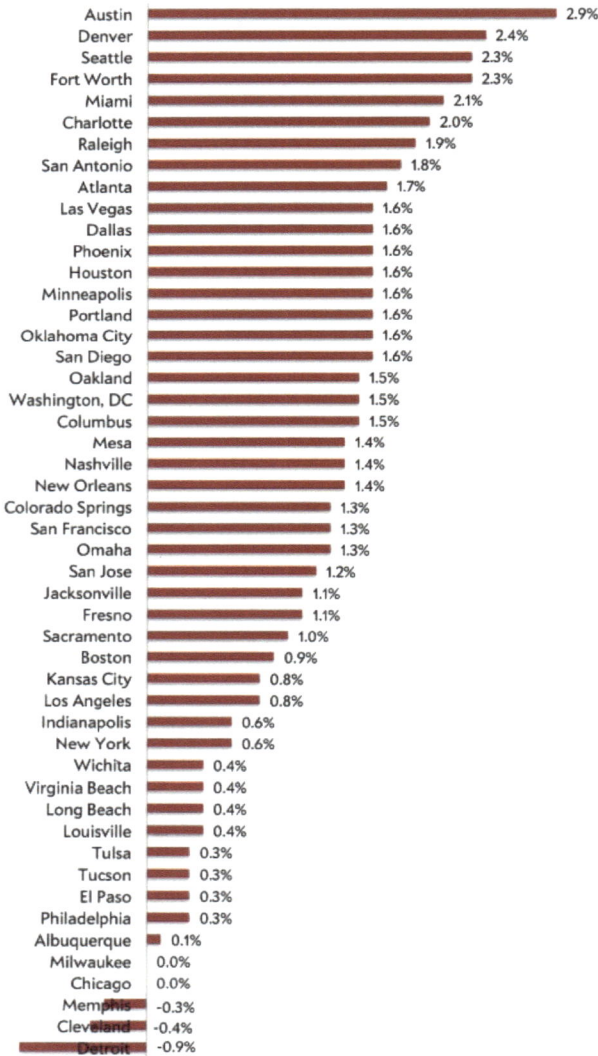

Austin	2.9%
Denver	2.4%
Seattle	2.3%
Fort Worth	2.3%
Miami	2.1%
Charlotte	2.0%
Raleigh	1.9%
San Antonio	1.8%
Atlanta	1.7%
Las Vegas	1.6%
Dallas	1.6%
Phoenix	1.6%
Houston	1.6%
Minneapolis	1.6%
Portland	1.6%
Oklahoma City	1.6%
San Diego	1.6%
Oakland	1.5%
Washington, DC	1.5%
Columbus	1.5%
Mesa	1.4%
Nashville	1.4%
New Orleans	1.4%
Colorado Springs	1.3%
San Francisco	1.3%
Omaha	1.3%
San Jose	1.2%
Jacksonville	1.1%
Fresno	1.1%
Sacramento	1.0%
Boston	0.9%
Kansas City	0.8%
Los Angeles	0.8%
Indianapolis	0.6%
New York	0.6%
Wichita	0.4%
Virginia Beach	0.4%
Long Beach	0.4%
Louisville	0.4%
Tulsa	0.3%
Tucson	0.3%
El Paso	0.3%
Philadelphia	0.3%
Albuquerque	0.1%
Milwaukee	0.0%
Chicago	0.0%
Memphis	-0.3%
Cleveland	-0.4%
Detroit	-0.9%

AMERICA'S MOST SUSTAINABLE CITY

Among the reasons why Austin is being touted as America's "most sustainable city" is its extensive use of bicycles and shared mini cars all over the downtown area. There is even talk of establishing a tram system.

One of the many smart cars in Austin. Source: Eric Kaufman (2016)

One of the many bike stations throughout Austin under the Austin Bicycle program.
Source: Eric Kaufman (December 2016)

Still, the City of Austin must develop its mass transportation system to meet the needs of the over 2 million living in the Austin metro area. Currently there is only one light rail system. Cap Metro operates a 26-mile long service from downtown Austin travelling northward through the suburbs to the town of Leander.

Austin is also developing strategies to utilize the enormous amount of rainwater generated by its heavy rainstorms – as much as 12 inches of rain can fall in one day. The clay soil prevents such rainwater from being absorbed and instead produces a large volume of run-off water and flooding. You can see rain barrels being used in varying degrees at residential areas; these barrels act like the cisterns of ancient times to capture and reuse rain water. But when these rain barrels remain open to the air, the standing water in them can grow stagnant and attract mosquitos, leading to disease.

Austin also has a purple pipe system, dedicated for recycling wastewater for irrigation and toilets. It is extending this system and its use through such requirements as any development within 200 feet of the purple pipe must access it. Measures like this will make reusing water a way of life.

CHALLENGES OF GROWTH

The city relies heavily on an aquifer that is being depleted partially because of increased consumption due to population growth and the lack of rain needed to replenish the aquifer. There is also evidence that single-family homes have higher water usage due to outdoor usage and landscape irrigation and other factor than in multifamily buildings.[110]

As discussed, by 2050 the population of Austin metropolitan region is estimated to reach about 3.7 million people. To accommodate this increase would likely require combining Unincorporated Austin – a 300 square mile area or a span of five miles outside of the existing city limits – to the 300 square miles of Austin for a total of 600 square miles.

The capacity to accommodate the current and future population inflows will require a multi-tier strategy that expands mass transit and provides affordable housing. "We need a combination of property tax relief, broader development of medium-density housing options, and funding for transportation projects to have a lasting impact on Central Texas affordability and infrastructure," said Barb Cooper of the Austin Board of Realtors.[111] The recently enacted Proposition 7 increases funding into the State Highway Fund for "building, maintaining and restoring non-tolled public roads and repaying transportation-related debt."[112] For now it appears the authorizing language of the legislation does not provide for extension of the mass transit system.

Higher-density housing as well has to be constructed to create more affordable options and increase the quantity needed. And as already mentioned multi-family and higher-density housing have less outdoors space that requires high water usage.

Austin also needs a more comprehensive approach and long-term plan to water management – a system that includes water sourcing, water conservation and water harvesting. Right now, the City relies on the Lower Colorado River Authority (LCRA) to provide some of its supplemental water under a long-term contract until 2100. This contract is conditioned upon Lake Travis not going below 30% of its reservoir capacity as Austin relies first and foremost on its system of lakes. LCRA is also servicing six states (in addition to Texas) and two Mexican states.[113] Its ability to do this is compromised during extended periods of severe drought conditions.

Meeting the transit needs of Austin will be a challenge. Source: Eric Kaufman (2016)

Development and implementation of a multi-tier strategy recommended by Cooper of the Austin Board of Realtors will require coordinated and long-term commitment among its various municipal departments. As it stands, Marc Coudert, who is responsible for resilience planning at the City of Austin, explained that departments have different planning horizons. The fire and police departments have one-year planning horizon; the water department a five-year planning horizon; and planners a 20-year planning horizon. These time frames do not look past 2036 much less plan for the pivotal year of 2050.

For us, 2050 is a critical time period as the human population is expected to reach 9 billion and sea level rise will also increase exponentially especially if carbon emissions are not stabilized or reduced. Under these circumstances, food, water and energy supplies will become a top priority.

View from Town Lake bike and hiking path. Source: Eric Kaufman (November 2016)

Austin Downtown Bike Share Program. Source: Eric Kaufman (April 2016)

CHAPTER **16**

CASE STUDY: ABANDONED COAL-MINING TOWNS, WEST VIRGINIA

Many former coal-mining towns in West Virginia have become historic landmark sites visited by thousands each year. What is drawing these numbers of visitors?

For the most part, these towns are in very rural locations, with railroad access, mountainous terrains, mostly green topography and a river often flowing through or near them. These factors, along with being picturesque, make them potential sites for low-density relocation communities at elevations above sea level where food can be produced and water supply exist.

We envision locating these self-sustainable, resilient relocation communities within a day's walk of each other – clustering them around the existing railroad system. The rail system, once upgraded, can link these areas to relatively larger centers. But it remains to be determined whether former coal-mining sites in areas like the New River Gorge (in the southern central portion of the state) and those in the northern part of the state near Pennsylvania suffer from lasting, continuing damage to air and water quality and whether such damage can be addressed in a cost-effective manner.

For three days in October of 2016, Eric explored the New River Gorge area and some of the partially and fully abandoned former coal-mining and railroad depot towns of Thurmond and Stotesbury and others along Route 16S, as well as existing coal-mining towns. His photos should give you a sense of the area's natural beauty and potential as relocation communities.

New River Gorge, WV. An existing coal-mining town on Route 16S.
Source: Eric Kaufman (October 2016)

Charlestown, WV. Protected farmland.
Source: Eric Kaufman (October 2016)

In addition to the extensive coal-mining activities throughout the New River Gorge, rampant clear cutting of ancient forests (a practice often equated with deforestation) provides another source of income. Such activity is harming air and water quality. The Nature Conservancy has indicated that 95% of the Red Spruce forests in Central Appalachia have been clear-cut.

One solution through this is for the Federal government to determine the actual number of people who depend upon coal mining for a living in West Virginia; then re-deploy these people into re-growing forests as well as retrain them in the production of solar panels and wind turbines. Establishing data centers in these areas of West Virginia also seems worth pursuing due to their relatively isolated location and proximity to areas like Washington DC. In both cases, incentives structured to attract tech and manufacturing companies to train and employ West Virginians would produce a win-win solution for companies and residents. Using these type of incentives to shift behavior away from coal-mining and clear-cutting practices serves as a downpayment towards establishing a sustainable economy and a pathway for creating new jobs, stimulating economic growth and empowering people around community, innovation, technology and manufacturing.

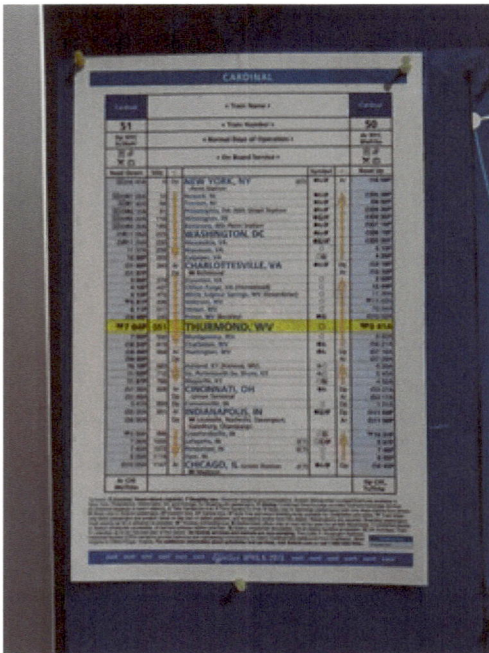

Thurmond, WV Amtrak Train Schedule.
Source: Eric Kaufman (October 2016)

New River Gorge Bridge completed in 1977.
Source: Eric Kaufman (October 2016)

As it is, three important trends within the coal industry are having a particularly harsh impact on West Virginia: the decrease in coal-mining jobs; the high cost of coal-mining jobs; and the lower productivity of mines in the eastern parts of the country as compared to ones located in the western areas. Coal-producing companies are increasingly facing the need to reduce their cost structure particularly given the pressure to produce coal in a more environmentally friendly manner.

Decline in Coal-Mining Jobs

According to the Center for Media and Democracy that publishes SourceWatch, only 49,504 underground coal-mining jobs remain in the U.S as compared to the 159 million jobs available in the entire civilian labor force; as such permanent blue-collar coal industry employees represent a little more than 0.03% of the U.S. workforce.[114]

Since 1900, technological developments in the coal-mining industry have dramatically increased miner productivity; so while U.S. coal production is currently at a record high, the mining population needed is a fraction of what was needed during the height of coal mining during the 1910's and 20's.

Average coal power plant employment has fallen dramatically over the past few decades due to technological developments and rising labor costs.

High Cost of Coal-Mining Jobs

The average age of coal plant workers is 48 years. Krishnan and Associates concluded that "a 2,000 MW coal-fired plant with about 200 to 250 employees will likely lose half its current plant staff in the next decade due to retirement, attrition and other similar issues."[115]

The average age of coal miners in West Virginia is 55.[116]

The average earnings of nonsupervisory coal workers in 2006 was $1,093 per week or $22.08 per hour as compared to average nonsupervisory worker earnings in other industries of $568 per week or $16.76 per hour.[117]

In the coal, metal ore and nonmetallic mineral mining industries, 19 percent of workers were union members in 2006, compared with 12 percent of workers throughout private industry.

Western U.S. Mines Outperform Eastern Ones

A huge discrepancy in coal mining productivity exists between Western and Eastern U.S. mines. Montana (with 942 coal miners) produces more coal than Virginia (with 5,262 coal miners); Wyoming (with 5,837 coal miners) produces more coal than West Virginia, Kentucky, Pennsylvania, Virginia, Alabama and Illinois combined (with a total of 58,995 coal miners).[118]

The coal-mining industry has been moving its production to these Western states (especially to the Powder River Basin). It has dramatically cut its workforce in Appalachia, including West Virginia.

The amount of federal subsidies to the coal industry including use of federal land is not transparent,[119] but by some accounts over $70 billion have been provided since 1950 to 2009.[120] If we assume that each of the 49,504 jobs in the coal industry received a subsidy of $75,000 including benefits, this would total $4.245 billion in employment subsidies. In 2006 when there were a lot more coal miners employed, there were 20,000 jobs in West Virginia. With this $75,000 per job subsidy, this translates into an annual subsidy of $1.5 billion for West Virginia.

If this subsidy were not provided – with the understanding that these 20,000 coal-mining jobs were lost – we could re-deploy this workforce into renewable energy technology and clean up the former and existing coal-mining communities in West Virginia, Pennsylvania and parts of upstate New York. Of course, this idea would not be politically popular but it is the kind of plan that would meet the triple bottom line of economic, social and environmental benefits – and would really prepare these communities for the near and distant future.

Can we devise a better economic and job-creating model that utilizes this subsidy (likely now less than $1.5 billion) for West Virginia's coal-mining jobs to instead revitalize, rebuild and create a series of vibrant new communities in this state? Can we establish dynamic public-private partnerships between the government, tech, real estate and renewable energy and fossil fuel (that include existing coal) industries that work towards building a sustainable and resilient economy? Rather than accelerating the pace of carbon emission, can we promote an energy-efficient, green economy? Can we also envision these communities as growing into relocation cities for people displaced in storms resulting from climate change in gulf state areas like Baton Rouge and New Orleans, Louisiana, and middle Atlantic Coastal areas like the Chesapeake Bay and the Carolina Outer Banks?

As we redirect these federal subsidies towards a strong, green economy, we can also utilize the resources of the National Park Service to thoroughly clean up these towns and establish them as relocation cities. Here we envision that the population of West Virginia can be doubled from its current 1.8 million to 3.6 million residents by the year 2050. The areas of New River Gorge, Charlestown and Harpers Ferry with their "good bones" can be transformed to support increased population with a good quality of life for existing and new residents.

Stotesbury, WV. Largely abandoned coal-mining town with this church still in operation. Source: Eric Kaufman (October 2016)

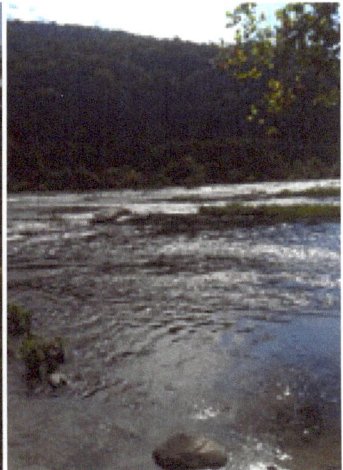

Sunset at the New River Gorge, West Virginia (left), and Harpers Ferry, WV recreation area (right). Source: Eric Kaufman (October 2016)

Thurmond, WV. Former active coal rail in town with historic significance. Source: Eric Kaufman (October 2016)

The New River Gorge Area of southwest West Virginia.
Source: Eric Kaufman (October 2016)

Nutallburg, West Virginia Abandoned coal-mining town with
company store. Source: Eric Kaufman (October 2016)

Nutallburg, WV. Abandoned coal mining equipment in New River Gorge area.
Source: Eric Kaufman (October 2016)

CHAPTER 17
CASE STUDY: CARTAGENA, BOLIVAR, COLOMBIA

Cartagena Skyline. Source: Arlen Stawasz

The Cartagena population has its origins with native pre-Colombian Indians. Spain colonized the area around 1533 A.D. Because of the colonial period and slave importation, the people of Cartagena are a mixture of pre-Colombian Indian, African and European ancestry.

Reflective of its long history, Cartagena has been designated by UNESCO a world heritage site due to its rich colonial style architecture and the remnants of a walled city constructed during the 1600's and 1700's to protect the city against pirates.

THE OLD CITY AND BOCAGRANDE

Cartagena in its entirety has an average elevation of 1 meter or 3 feet above sea level. The city of Cartagena and its walled complex (called the Old City) are best characterized as forming a coastal city where it faces the Caribbean Sea to the west and a lagoon or marsh called Cienaga de la Virgen (Virgin Marsh) to its southeast side. Extending south from the old city is Bocagrande, a true peninsula that juts out into the Caribbean Sea on its west and the Cartagena Bay to its east.

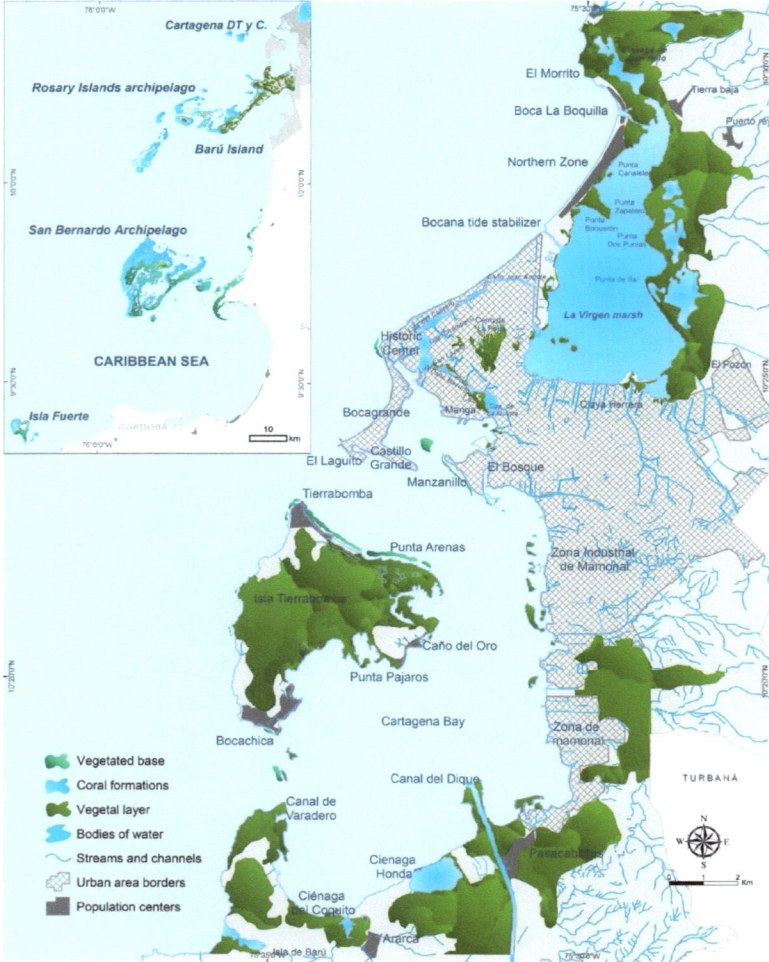

Detailed Map of Cartagena. Source: Cartagena Plan 4C

The city of Cartagena and its surrounding environs currently have about 1 million inhabitants and are projected to double in population by 2050. The combination of Old World colonial architecture and modern hotels nearby has made Cartagena a compelling tourism and vacation home success story. Tourism is one of Cartagena's biggest industries; it is visited by people from around the world and is a popular holiday destination for those within the country. Christmas and other holidays are especially popular periods for tourists, with traffic jams being the norm. Unfortunately, without measures to curb development focused on short-term opportunities without due consideration of the long-term impact, this treasure of an asset may become a natural water park as the sea reclaims this gem for its own.

Up until the 1940's, the land just south of the walled Old City was a very sleepy vacation haven for wealthy Colombians who largely resided in Bogota and used Cartagena as a summer and winter retreat. In the 1990's, local and foreign developers began major hotel development on the waterfront. They created this area now known as Bocagrande as a haven for tourists. Since 2005, however, the federal Colombian government has been aware of the risks that sea level rise poses to Cartagena.

View from the Old City overlooking Bocagrande.
Source: Eric Kaufman (2016)

Cartagena, Colombia. Flooding of Old Town without
any rainfall. Source: Facebook

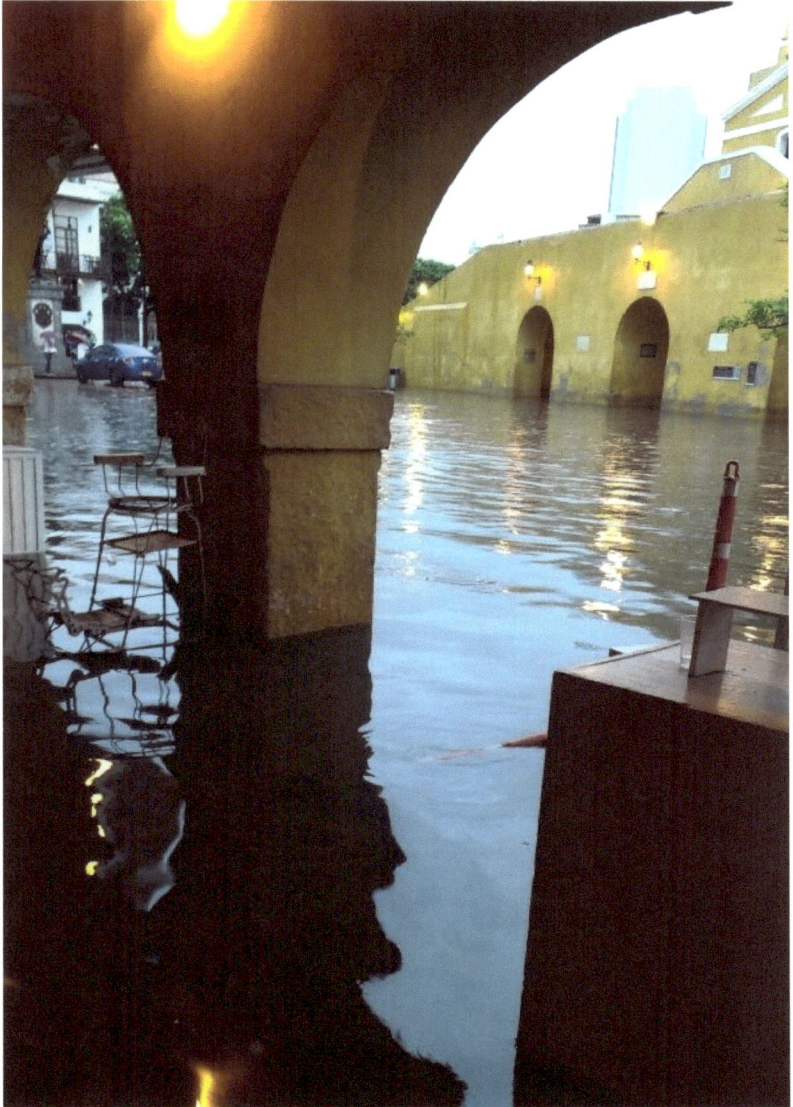

Cartagena, Colombia. Flooding of Old Town.
Source: Facebook

PROTECTING AGAINST SEA LEVEL RISE

Both the city of Cartagena and Bocagrande flood even when it does not rain — a situation not unlike that of South Miami Beach. This occurs because the hotels were largely constructed at sea level, without any resilience measures built into the construction. Like many coastal areas, as there has not been a major flood in quite a while, people cope with this "nuisance flooding" and are less concerned with a potential catastrophic situation.

Cartagena's resilience challenges are further complicated by its rainy season, being surrounded by water and the inadequate sewage drainage system allowing water to collect where mosquitos reproduce and can cause dengue fever.

Natural adaptation measures include restoring mangroves though this can only be a partial solution to the more endemic problem of the sea literally encroaching on Cartagena. The restoration of coral reefs would serve as natural berms; these efforts as well will only be temporary and not sufficient for the long-term. Instead it appears only the eventual relocation of people upland into sustainable, resilient communities (still to be established) is the full-scale solution. But for many people who love this area, for the moment relocation is considered an impossible thought.

Then there is a form of Klaus Jacob's nomadic infrastructure such as houses and structures built on stilts called palafitos — structures built over lakes and lagoons. These palafitos found in Cartagena have also been used in ancient lakes in Switzerland and other parts of northern Europe.

Mangroves as a natural barrier against sea level rise.
Source: Stock Image

Example of houses built on stilts (palafitos).
Source: Stock Image

The long-term solution of eventual relocation upland to more sustainable and resilient communities can also provide housing for many – 100,000 or so people – living in abject poverty.[121] Among the most notorious of these poverty-stricken areas is "Boston," a neighborhood where squatters have "established" makeshift residences and the city provided water and electric metering in most instances.

FIRST CLIMATE ADAPTATION PLAN IN COLOMBIA

In Colombia, Cartagena is the first coastal city to develop an adaptation plan called Plan 4C – Una Cartagena Competitiva y Compatible con el Clima – or a Plan for a Competitive, Climate-Compatible Cartagena. They began this initiative as the public and private sectors began to realize that their developments have not been thus far resilient. In fact, one of Eric's colleagues has observed that Cartagena is "the poster child for how not to do climate adaptation planning" – especially with its most recent development in Bocagrande.

Unfortunately Plan 4C is not finished and needs over $500,000 to complete the planning phase; this does not include the funding needed to implement the adaptation measures Plan 4C lays out for the inevitable sea level rise. Plan 4C seeks to engage, among its objectives, the tourism sector to help with resilience planning. This sector includes major hotel chains like Intercontinental and Sofitel, whose business interests it would seem would be, first and foremost, to ensure their visitors are safe. But to date, the tourism and hotel developers have not offered their support nor undertaken to fund the completion of Plan 4C.

NEED FOR AN EVACUATION PLAN

We see there is a need for providing a viable evacuation plan for the walled sections of the city as well as the non-walled sections on the seashore or along any water body. Each time it rains, the city floods, from the north – where the poorest sections of Cartagena are located – along and southerly – towards the high-end neighborhoods of Bocagrande and Castillo Grande – connected only by the Avenida Santander along the shores of the Virgen Marshes (Cienaga de la Virgen). The narrow streets, which already do not allow for an easy flow of cars and pedestrians, would be overwhelmed should there be a need to evacuate the city during an extreme weather event.

Diego Bermúdez, a landscape architect, has developed a viable regional plan that includes Cartagena with its population of nearly 1 million people, Barranquilla and its nearly 2 million residents, and Santa Marta and its 500,000 people. Like Cartagena, these cities are also expected to double in population by 2050. His plan addresses the challenges of providing additional housing and the anticipated rise in sea levels and flooding.

Along the same vein, we see that the areas to the east of Cartagena (Turbaco and Turbana) have much higher elevations ranging from 60 to 174 meters (200 feet plus) and seem ideal as evacuation sites as well as relocation sites where sustainable, resilient communities can be built for both these potential evacuees and to accommodate the increased projected population.

REDIBUJANDO LA INFRAESTRUCTURA

TREN REGIONAL DE PASAJEROS
[2013] 4.2 millones habitantes + 3.6 millones visitantes/año
[2050] 6 millones de habitantes + 10 millones visitantes/año

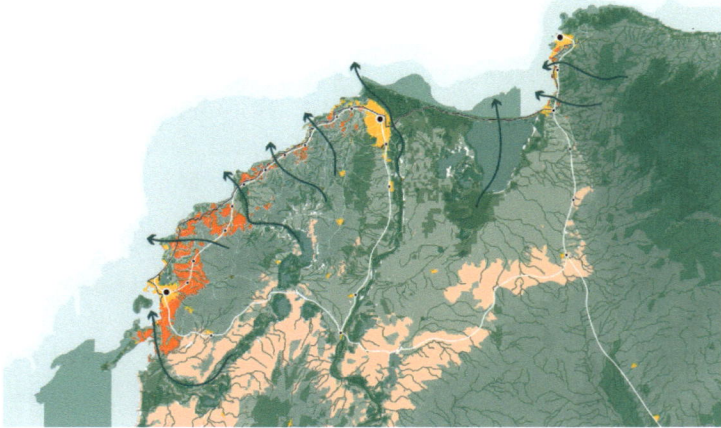

AREAS PARA DESARROLLO URBANO

350km²
A 10,000 personas/km2
La región podría hospedar 3.5 millones de habitantes nuevos

Con 2.5 millones de personas hoy
Para un total de 6.0 millones = proyección estimada 2050

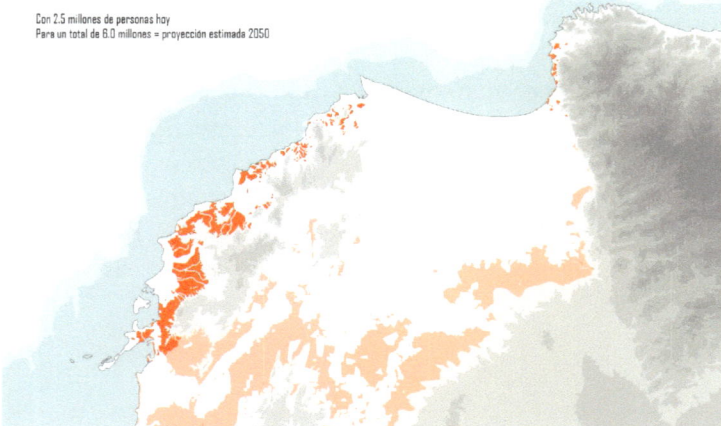

Top Map: Redrawing the Regional Train Infrastructure.   Bottom Map:
Areas Marked for Urban Population Growth. Source: Diego Bermúdez

CHAPTER 18
MAPS OF THE
GREAT CLIMATE DIASPORA

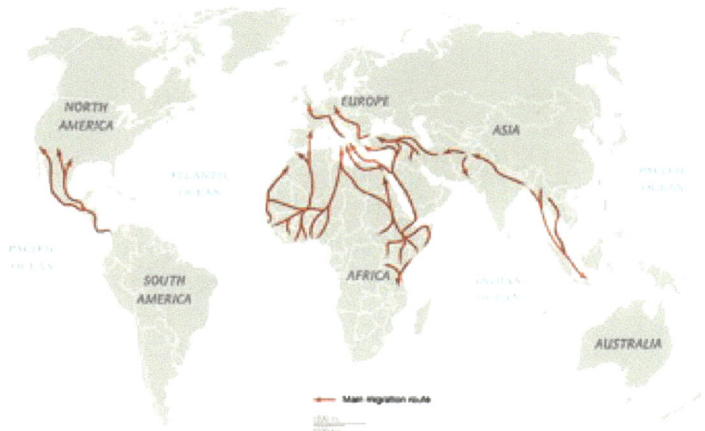

Source: National Geographic

The maps above and in the following pages depict the largely
northerly direction of present and anticipated migration: populations in South and Central America will migrate to the United

States and eventually Canada while those of Africa and the Middle East will migrate towards Europe. Already we are experiencing signs of these major human migration patterns, which will continue to accelerate in the next several decades.

Source: National Geographic

Under a framework of resource capitalism, we would deploy financial, technology and material resources to those countries that lie within these paths of human migration. Taken to its logical eventuality, countries like Greenland and areas like Siberia near the North Pole are projected to become fertile areas and, given their size, can house large numbers of people over the next several hundred years. Countries like Romania, Bulgaria and Czechoslovakia are in the direct path of human migration from the south so they also seem ripe for sustainable and resilient development during this period. See Appendix F for a partial list of countries and areas that would make sense for deployment of additional resources to accommodate the climate diaspora.

Source: National Geographic

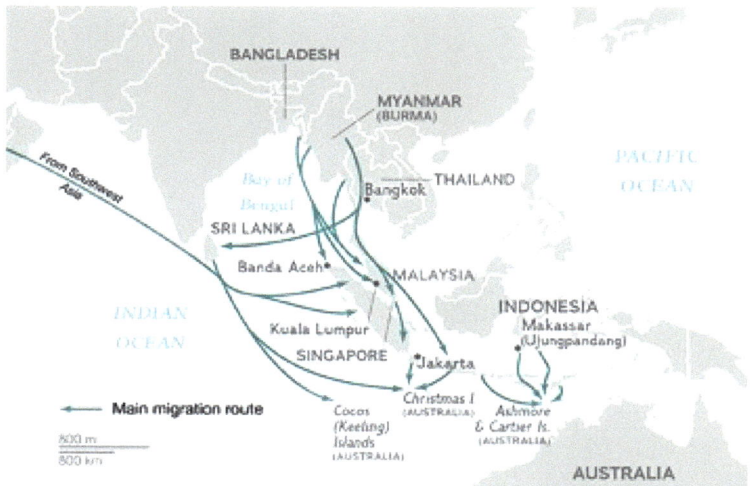

Source: National Geographic

The previous map shows rare north to south migrations – from Bangladesh due to difficulties entering countries like India and China. Still the migration from Bangladesh to Bangkok and Sri Lanka will be, we believe, temporary relocations to the small Australian-controlled islands of Christmas, Keeling (also known as Cocos Islands and Keeling Islands) and Ashmore & Cartier. These uninhabited islands will likely serve as stopovers for migrants to later fly to other more hospitable locations northward.

CHAPTER 19
ONE CONSERVATIVE'S TAKE ON PLAN RELOCATION

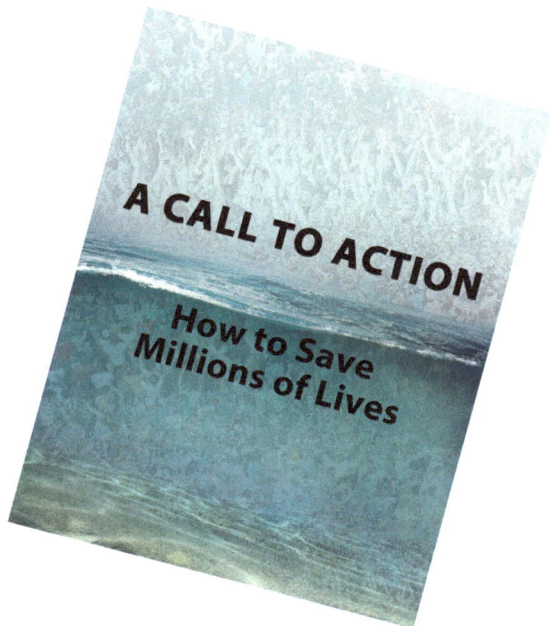

Eric asked his friend Parker S. Shannon, a political and fiscal conservative, to consider the possible impact of global warming and from "scratch" create a relocation plan. As an entrepreneur working with disruptive innovation strategies, Parker accepted the challenge. We include Parker's plan as something quite acceptable as it would acknowledge the general concept for a need of a Plan for Relocation. Alternatively, the stakes involved in saving the human species are too high to set one plan over another. At this point, such plans need to be made operational in preparation for The Great Climate Diaspora.

We invite readers such as you to do the same and participate in this Call to Action. Share your ideas on what Plan Relocation should look like by posting your comments on the NRF website, http://www.natresilience.org. Also feel free to send us requests on related topics, sustainable and resilient technologies you are interested in, and communities where you think there are opportunities to establish relocation communities. Depending on your comments, we may follow up with another book!

Parker Shannon's Summary

This potential road map for Plan R starts with the assumption that anything is possible. This model chooses not to deal with the Global Migration portion of a Climate Diaspora, but instead proposes Intra-Country Relocations (relocations within a country) as the first course of action. Any global migration issues are left for other discussions. Also, left for another discussion is any quantitative cost benefit analysis of avoiding climate disasters.

Key Assumptions

First, the net present value of $1,000 in 50 years (around 2066) will be worth only $8 today if that amount grows 10% each year. Second, most infrastructure assets will need to be replaced / repaired in 50 years, so at that future time, their remaining value will be small. Third, the future cost of climate change is something very real, which needs to be avoided, despite these first two present value calculations.

Fourth, this model identifies lands that the government could utilize as sites for relocation communities and cities. In the United States, the federal government owns about 640 million acres, of which 47% of such federal owned properties are located west of the Mississippi. The 50 states within the country collectively own an additional 14 million acres. Finally, there are 83 million acres of National Parks situated throughout every state except Delaware as well as an additional 14 million acres of State Parks.

Nations that do not own an amount of land sufficient for such relocation communities and cities should begin "land banking" in the event of sea levels rising. In any case, whether in the U.S. or in other countries, ideal properties to select and land bank for use as relocation communities and cities should have desirable elevations and access to food and water. Land banking policies may incorporate eminent domain, should minimize dislocation, and prohibit market manipulation and speculation.

<u>Fifth</u>, the U.S. can access nearly $2.5 trillion in corporate profits earned by Fortune 500 Corporations. Under a new national tax policy, the government could target and repatriate these profits and use them as investment capital to create relocation communities and cities, with the creation of a vast number of jobs being a positive outcome.

Parameters

<u>Create Universal Jobs</u>. The success of any Plan R as implemented will depend on the number of jobs created during the process of establishing these relocation communities and cities. If the global community reaches agreement on concepts like "universal income" and "population control," our leaders should certainly entertain a more meaningful and effective policy of creating "universal jobs." Simply put, universal jobs must be made available as part of these Plan R sustainable, resilient communities and cities. Universal jobs will be the catalyst for migration and vital source for economic well-being.

<u>Local Means of Production and a Policy of Free Access replaces Free Trade</u>. Such jobs need to come full circle where, as in the past, the means of production is located near the end consumer. The world can no longer accept the free movement of factories (and jobs) to any place in the globe that offers the lowest wages and best tax incentives. Before we had operated on the assumption that products could be easily shipped to consumers around the world. Now we would want to avoid a gaming scenario where the location experiencing critical decay due to climate change offers the lowest wages, grants the best tax incentives and, otherwise, manipu-

lates their currency and local tax policy. Critical decay can affect large areas of a particular state and even major sections of a country. Such gaming practices would undermine the effectiveness of this relocation plan. Instead, globalization under this plan requires the end of "free trade" and the start of "free access." Under this policy of free access, multinational corporations must build complete factories in each of the G20 countries to employ the consumers to whom and in the countries where they plan to sell their products.

New Global Treaties. This concept of lifting incomes through job creation is not much different from The Marshall Plan developed by the United States to rebuild Europe after WWII. Global leaders must now rewrite global treaties, which, for example, would provide a job-creating plan in each country's Plan R city; establish green factories; and create green cities that offer a better lifestyle within a sustainable environment.

The United Nations must champion global treaties on taxes and trade access. The Global Treaty on Taxes and Currencies would eliminate currency manipulation and standardize an effective tax rate between all nations. This would eliminate the current "beggar thy neighbor" tax policy which encourages "tax inversions" (moving jobs to the cheapest tax rate) and the $2.5 trillion in un-repatriated corporate profits which are draining jobs from the United States. If corporate taxes and currencies were equal in all countries, then the largest corporate expense would be transportation. As such corporate self-interest would dictate moving their factories (and jobs) closest to the consumer. On this basis, we can create the "universal job" and universal wages.

The Global Treaty on Trade Access would eliminate the existing barriers preventing global corporations from building factories in local countries. Current free trade treaties focus on the shipment of goods and services between countries; but these free access treaties would focus on the production of goods and services around the globe, and within each country of their customer base.

Finally, there must be a Managed Plan for Climate Affected Cities and New Sister Cities. Under this plan the federal government will give a land grant in a location that will be designated as a Sister City for a specific climate-affected city. Essentially, businesses, residents and operations of the climate-affected city would relocate to the Sister City. In this process, property and business owners would exchange their land deeds and business interests in the climate-affected city into the new Sister City as "homesteaders."[122] In this exchange, they will give up or forfeit their deeds of properties and businesses in the climate-affected city for new property in the Sister City. These Sister Cities and the new jobs and factories will be financed and created from the incentives provided under another treaty – the United Nations Treaty on Taxes and Trade Access to global corporations – and the $2.5 trillion the federal government repatriated from overseas profits.

The climate-affected city and its new Sister City will be part of the same municipality, which will align the interests of both cities and manage the migration from old to new communities. The Internet of everything, digital technology and distance learning allow for and will facilitate the management by the same municipality of the two cities. In addition, the municipality will manage both cities to ensure the flow and utilization of resources including existing tax proceeds in the climate-affected city to support the new Sister City.

Parker argues that climate-affected cities face the risk of critical decay. Like stranded assets, the municipality will experience a loss of its usable lands due to the impact of extreme weather events, which, combined with the necessary migration of its tax base, threatens that city's continued existence. He believes it would be in the best interest of these climate-affected cities to prevent reaching that condition of critical decay by undertaking this Plan R.

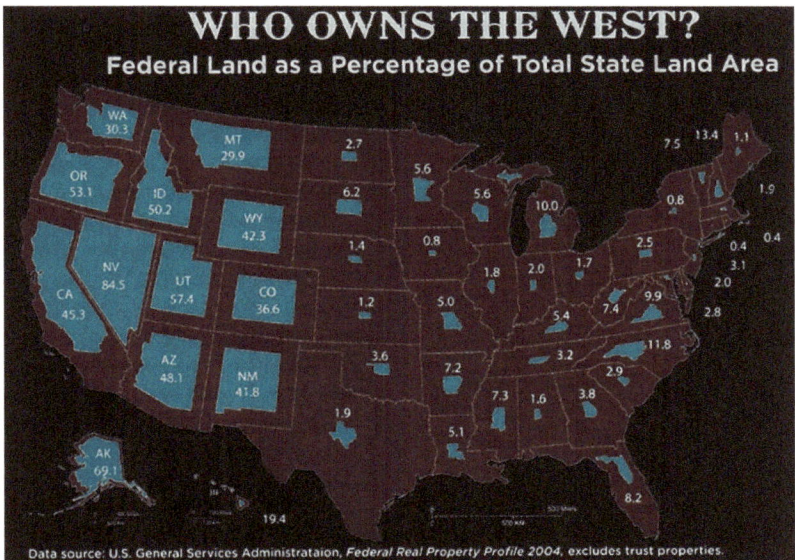

U.S. General Services Administration Federal Real Property Profile 2004 excludes trust properties

CHAPTER 20
EPILOGUE

A discussion about the effects of climate change inevitably involves people asking – "So when is this going to happen?"

The answer is – We do not know . . .

No one can predict when the impact of climate change will occur or how strong it will be; moreover, its impact will vary around the globe, within countries and their individual regions. Consider this analogy used by some to highlight the problem faced by humanity.

> A frog when placed in boiling water immediately knows to jump out of the water to escape its death. On the other hand, a frog placed in simmering water, which is slowly growing to a boil, remains in that water because it does not immediately feel the effects of the temperature rise. And so, the frog remains in the water until it is too late.

The frog in this instance is we, humans. We all are in a slow boiling pot called earth, experiencing the effects of global warming. At what point will such climate change become unbearable, or will we have become used to the worsening conditions at a point tragically too late to make a change? Those of us living in the developed world have this luxury and, in some respects, the burden of avoidance and denial.

We end this book with **A Call to Action** that opens a discussion on this and other questions for you the reader and our collective humanity to decide. What type of world do we want to leave our children, grandchildren and future generations? Already our actions today are affecting millions in our country and, should we continue this present course of action, we may not be able to change course and save ourselves.

WHAT'S AT STAKE?

As we have discussed throughout this book, one key aspect of climate change is its effect on rising sea levels. James-Robert provides certain maps and scenarios in this section to give a real sense of how rising sea levels would, for example, affect coastal areas in terms of loss of homes and other property, loss of utilities and, most significantly, loss of lives.

The following map of the United States demonstrates which coastal states are most vulnerable to the effects of sea level rise. The one magenta-colored and three orange-colored states – Florida, Louisiana, New York and California – have the greatest number of vulnerable residents living in low-lying coastal areas at less than 3.3 feet above high tide.

The Union of Concerned Scientists established 3.3 feet as the global average of sea level rise under an intermediate-high projection – a measure between the intermediate-low range and highest SLR projection. This means anywhere from 2.1 million to 4.2 million people will be affected by and face increasing danger to themselves and their loved ones as well as damage to their homes and other properties.

Coastal States at Risk from Global Sea Level Rise[123]

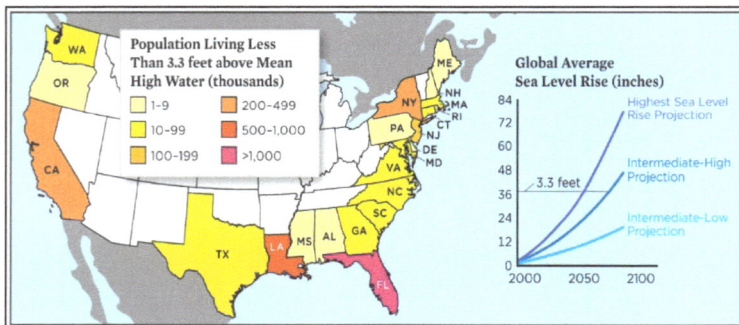

So whatever is your political leaning, as Sam Cooke sang "a change is gonna come,"[124] the question is by how much and how soon.

Lower Manhattan and Brooklyn (NY) and Jersey City (NJ)

To better understand how sea level rise will affect the lives of people in these low-lying areas, we consider how the Lower Manhattan / Brooklyn and Jersey City shorelines will be affected by increasing global temperatures and climate change. This analysis, prepared by a climate change think tank, Climate Central, also holds true for many other coastal areas like New Orleans, LA, and in Los Angeles, CA. You can access the Climate Central website at http://www.sealevel.climatecentral.org select

Risk Zone Map and then enter the name of the location. Once you enter the map you can adjust the water level on the left to varying assumptions.

The scientists and journalists of Climate Central generated the following maps[125] to reflect the impact of four temperature rise scenarios in the Lower Manhattan / Brooklyn, NY and Jersey City, NJ waterfronts. Each temperature rise – be it an increase of 1.5° C (2.7° F), 2° C (3.6° F), 3° C (5.4° F) or an increase of 4° C (7.2° F) – flows from the decisions we will make over our collective carbon consumption.

New York[126]

The areas shaded in blue on the map on the next page depict those locations that will be permanently underwater. The difference between the 1.5° C (2.7° F) and the 4° C (7.2° F) scenario is dramatic. First, the area underwater will nearly triple with the water moving inward from the coast regions. Second, virtually all the coastal areas will be underwater.

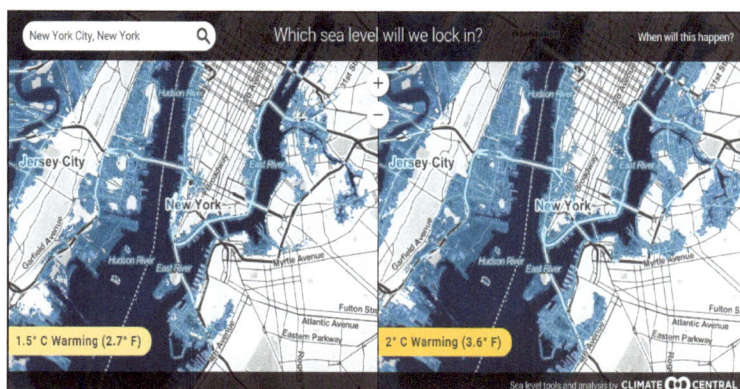

Climate Central provides a different but related look at the impact of rising seas, this time within the State of New York. It
zeros in on the most affected areas identified by zip code in its
report "New York and the Surging Sea."[127] We reproduced and
simplified their table.[128] What you immediately see is that the
five zip codes most affected depending on which measure you
use – number of people, amount of property value, number of
housing units – are all located in New York City in three of its
boroughs, Manhattan, Brooklyn and Queens.

Climate Central Top Zip Codes at Risk below 9 Ft

Group	State total below 9ft of water	Top 5 zip codes affected below 9ft of water	5 Zip Codes Most Affected
Amount of Land (acres)	118,737	12,878	JFK Airport, Massapequa, Southampton, East Hampton, Amagansett
Population	930,270	234,094	Manhattan Beach, Coney Island and Canarsie in Brooklyn; Long Beach, Manhattan; Far Rockaway, Queens
Housing Units	404,952	101,502	Manhattan Beach, Coney Island and Canarsie in Brooklyn; Long Beach, Manhattan; Far Rockaway, Queens
Property Value	$176 billion	$26.9 billion	Manhattan Beach and Mill Basin in Brooklyn; Long Beach and Battery Park City in Manhattan; Rockaway Park, Queens

At an SLR of 9 feet, the impact on New York State is serious: $176 billion in property value with 118,737 acres and close to a million people affected. The top five zip code and communities affected within the state are all in NYC with $26.9 billion in property value, 12,878 acres and 234,094 people all at risk.

New Orleans (LA)

Again courtesy of Climate Central, below are the same maps
and (four) temperature scenarios, this time, adjusted for New
Orleans. The areas shaded in blue depict those locations that
will be permanently underwater.   Under <u>any</u> temperature
change the Greater New Orleans metro area will be submerged
in water. But as temperature rises by 1.5° C (2.7° F) to 4° C
(7.2° F), the coastal areas north of the city are increasingly affected. For example, north of New Orleans running west to
east along I-12 are Ponchatoula, Hammond and Covington in
Louisiana, and Picayune in Mississippi, which were relatively
untouched under a 1.5° C (2.7° F) increase but are expected to
become submerged or face encroaching waters as the global
temperatures rise by 4° C (7.2° F).

New Orleans[129]

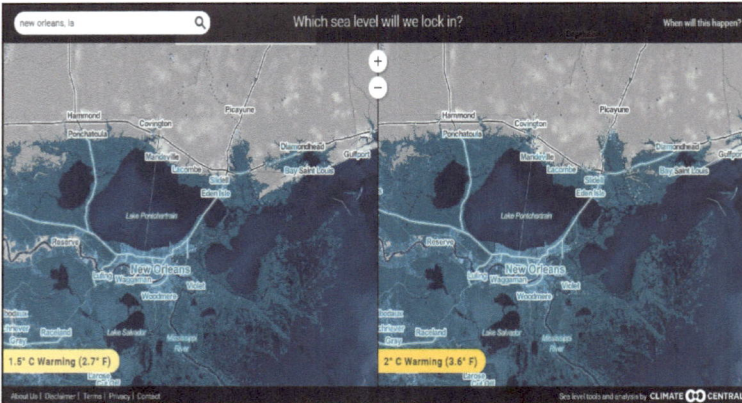

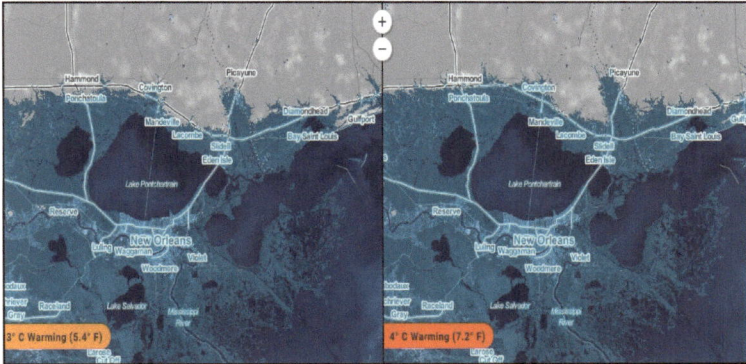

From the data provided by Climate Central in its New Orleans Report, at a 9-foot SLR the impact worsens with 339,294 or "98.8% of the population in New Orleans affected" along with 187,153 housing units and $27.6 billion in property value.[130]

Los Angeles (CA)

In our last example we examine Los Angeles, CA. Again the areas shaded blue depicts those locations that will be permanently underwater. The difference between the impact of 1.5° C (2.7° F) and 4° C (7.2° F) temperature increase is again dramatic with inland communities now affected.[131]

Los Angeles[132]

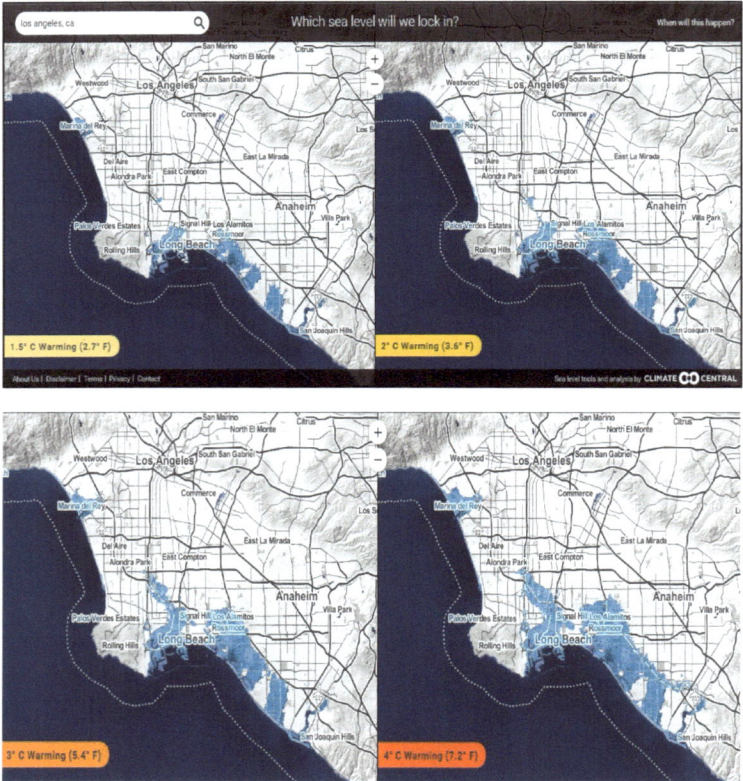

A CALL TO ACTION

We now have the ability to determine in some measure the direction our actions have on our earth. Rather than battling or thwarting the power of Mother Nature, we need to co-operate, co-exist and respect her power as being greater than our own (as a species). We should then act accordingly by instituting immediate, meaningful and positive changes in our lifestyle and economy.

Our call to action proposes three sets of actions. Each action will pave the way for significant economic development, the creation of numerous jobs, address the challenges faced by climate-affected communities while strengthening others. But undertaken simultaneously, we have a higher likelihood of generating a level of technological innovation needed to shift us to a non-fossil fuel-based economy. This innovation can lead to enjoying unparalleled opportunities for increasing domestic manufacturing and building, entrepreneurial activity and small business ownership.

Mother Nature may be giving us a real gift when we evolve with her and live in better harmony with our environment, our resources and ourselves. We only have to act.

Green Economy

Continue with establishing the green economy: create green jobs, reduce our carbon footprint and use renewable energy sources. Recycle, reuse and repurpose.

State Action

Each state works through its legislators, economists, climatologists and economic development experts to undertake and implement the following actions:

(1)   Identify the areas within the state that are most vulnerable to the effects of extreme weather or climate change;

(2)   Identify potential sites to establish relocation communities or cities; and

(3)   Develop an economic and tax package and implementation strategy constructed around PuPCos as appropriate.

Federal Action

(1)   Consider and respond to the findings of each state as to their climate-vulnerable locations.

(2)   Draw from scientific research on how to reduce health and environmental impacts from climate change and develop viable, cost-effective solutions for climate adaptation and resilience.

(3)   Utilize the resources of the Environmental Protection Agency, National Oceanic and Atmospheric Administration, and Centers for Disease Control and Prevention.

(4) Formulate and provide federal resources to establish relocation cities and communities. Resources can include potential relocation sites using federal properties, economic and tax incentives and credits and incentives structured around PuPCos.

GLOSSARY

Study this section to become conversant about climate change at cocktail parties and other important gatherings. We have liberally relied on and, therefore, must recognize and thank James Lovelock for his excellent glossary of terms in his book, *The Vanishing Face of Gaia – A Final Warning*.

Albedo

A measure used by astronomers of the amount of sunlight reflected by a planetary surface. Albedos range from 1 for complete reflection to 0 for complete absorption. The average for the earth's albedo is 0.33, but clouds and ice can approach 1.0 and the ocean is less than 0.2. More simply, more absorption (closer to 0) means more global heating.

Global heating reduces ice, snow and some cloud cover, which leads to lower planetary albedo and results in a positive feedback – a good application of this defined term as you can see below – of greater absorption of sunlight and even more global heating. The heat absorbed from sunlight is linked to the albedo, but that does not automatically make a dark forest warmer than the light-colored desert nearby. Most vegetation has a lower albedo than the planetary average but keeps cool by evaporating water from its leaves.[133]

Algae

These organisms use sunlight to make organic matter and oxygen. The first algae on earth appeared soon after life started over three billion years ago. Their form was bacterial and these microscopic organisms are still abundant. They are found either as free-living organisms or, importantly, as inclusions called chloroplasts within the more complex cells of plants.

Algae are unusually influential in the earth's climate as they remove carbon dioxide from the air and generate the gas dimethyl sulphide (DMS), which oxidizes in the air and become tiny nuclei that seed the cloud droplets. Fossilized algae are the source of petroleum. Algal farms may provide a future source of food and fuel.[134]

Aquifer

Porous rock, sediment, sand or gravel that is filled with water as water flows through them.

Atoll

A ring-shaped reef, island or chain of islands formed of coral.

Berms

These are mounds or walls of earth or sand. They can also be referred to as landscaped berm.

Biosphere

This is the geographical region of the earth where life is found. Now it is used as an imprecise word that acknowledges the power of life on earth without surrendering human sovereignty.[135]

Built Environment _____

"A material, spatial and cultural product of human labor that combines physical elements and energy in forms for living, working and playing . . . . The man-made surroundings that provide the setting for human activity, ranging in scale from buildings and parks or green spaces to neighborhoods and cities that can often include their supporting infrastructure, such as water supply or energy networks."[136]

The built environment includes cities, buildings, urban spaces, walkways, roads, parks, etc. The study of the built environment is interdisciplinary in nature and can include such disciplines as: visual arts, architecture, engineering, urban planning, history, interior design, industrial design, geography, environmental studies, anthropology and sociology.

Cap and Trade Mechanisms _____

These refer to an environmental and economic approach to controlling greenhouse gas emissions as the primary driver of global warming. The "cap" sets a limit on emissions or carbon allowances, which is lowered over time to reduce the amount of pollutants released into the atmosphere. The "trade" creates a market for carbon allowances, helping companies innovate to meet or come below their allocated limit. The less they emit, the less they pay, so it is in their economic incentive to pollute less.[137]

Carbon Capture and Storage ____

See carbon sequestration and storage (CSS).

Carbon Emissions

<u>See</u> carbon neutrality; carbon sequestration and storage; carbon tax. Also known as CO_2, this refer to a colorless, odorless and non-poisonous gas formed by combustion of carbon as well as by the respiration of living organisms. Emissions refer to the general release of such greenhouse gases and/or their precursors into the atmosphere over a specified area and period.[138]

Carbon Neutrality / Net Zero Carbon Footprint

<u>See</u> cap and trade mechanisms; carbon emissions; carbon tax; renewable energy. Carbon neutrality, also known as "net zero carbon footprint," seeks to manage and reduce carbon emissions. Thus far, there are two ways to implement this policy. First, "a measured amount of carbon released" is offset or balanced by "an equivalent amount" in renewable energy. In this way the overall reliance on fossil-fuel energy is reduced and compensated by an equivalent amount of renewable energy. The second approach is a market-based strategy utilizing cap and trade mechanisms (carbon credits, carbon trading, carbon tax and carbon offsetting).

Carbon Sequestration and Storage (CSS)

A technology that captures (sequesters) carbon emissions from the source of the carbon emitter like a power plant, then stores such emission underground.

Carbon Tax

A fee intended to make users of fossil fuels pay for climate damage their fuel use imposes by releasing carbon dioxide into the atmosphere and simultaneously motivate switching to cleaner energy. Because CO_2 is released in strict proportion to the fuel's carbon content, the carbon tax can be levied or imposed "upstream" on the fuel itself.[139]

Climate Change

This refers to any long-term change in the earth's climate or in the climate of a region or city. This includes warming, cooling and changes in climate in addition to temperature.

Climate Feedbacks

See positive and negative feedback. Positive feedbacks amplify the change in the first quantity while negative feedback reduces it. The term "forcing" means a change, which may "push" the climate system in the direction of warming or cooling. An example of a climate forcing is increased atmospheric concentrations of greenhouse gases.

Climate Resilience (Adaptation)

See resilience (adaptation).

COP21

COP21 was the 21st session of the Conference of the Parties to the United Nations Convention, organized by the United Nations. It was convened from November 30 to December 12, 2015 at the Paris-Le Bourget site. Every year since 1995, the

Conference of the Parties (COP) has gathered the 196 Parties (195 countries and the European Union), who ratified the Convention, to evaluate its implementation and negotiate new commitments.[140]

Corporate Resilience

Business resilience is the ability for an organization to quickly adapt to disruptions while maintaining continuous business operations and safeguarding people, assets and overall brand equity. Business resilience goes a step beyond disaster recovery by offering post-disaster strategies to avoid costly downtime, shore up vulnerabilities and maintain business operations in the face of additional, unexpected breaches.[141]

Corporate Social Responsibility (CSR)

This term refers to initiatives taken by a corporation to assess and take responsibility for the impact of its operations on the community and the environment. This applies to efforts that go beyond what may be required by regulators or environmental protection groups. CSR may also refer to a company's "corporate citizenship" and can involve incurring short-term costs that do not provide an immediate financial benefit to the company, but instead promote positive social and environmental change.

Corporatocracy

Corporatocracy refers to an economic and political system controlled by corporations or corporate interests. Economist Jeffrey Sachs used this term to describe the United States in *The Price of Civilization*.[142] The concept has been used in "explanations of bank bailouts, excessive pay . . . as well as complaints such as the exploitation of national treasuries, people and natural resources."[143]

Critical Decay _____

A term coined by Parker Shannon, a colleague of mine, indicating the point at which the loss of usable lands with the combined migration of its tax base threatens the continued viability of a municipality.

Deforestation _____

The cutting down and removal of all or most of the trees in a forested area. Deforestation can erode soils, contribute to desertification and the pollution of waterways, and decrease biodiversity through the destruction of habitat.[144]

Effect of the Melting of the Polar Ice Caps _____

The melting of the polar ice caps is caused by the overall increase in global temperature. This melting can have serious consequences for all organisms on earth. Besides being important for marine life, ice caps help regulate sea level and global temperatures. As polar ice caps are made of fresh water, their melting adds more fresh water that makes the ocean water less saline. This can cause problems for organisms that are well adapted to the very salty ocean waters.

EPPS Shift/ EPPS Syndrome _____

These terms, which Joaquin and I newly created, refer to the effect that our current structures, perspectives and viewpoints on economics, politics, psychology and sociology have on decision-making capacity. Our current interactions in our economy, politics, psychology and sociology form the constraints that constitute the EPPS Syndrome. A shift in our EPPS perspective is needed to allow us to work collectively to address climate change, hence the EPPS Shift.

Feedbacks, Positive Feedbacks ___

See climate feedbacks; positive and negative feedback.

Flood Gates / Flood Logs / Flood Panels _____

Increasingly, buildings have constructed temporary flood dams in the form of flood gates, flood logs and flood panels. Of course, these temporary measures are only effective when installed in time before the occurrence of the storm. Also FEMA officials during the aftermath of Sandy in the New York region "cautioned that a large number of these kinds of protection systems failed during Sandy."[145]

Gaia Hypothesis _____

During the early 1970s, James Lovelock and Lynn Margulis believed that life on earth actively keeps the surface conditions always favorable for whatever is the contemporary ensemble of organisms – simply put earth adapts to life. When introduced, this hypothesis was contrary to the conventional wisdom that life adapted to planetary conditions as it and they evolved in their separate ways.

Now we know that the hypothesis of earth adapts to life – a theory that has evolved into the Gaia Theory[146] – is incorrect as it is the whole earth system that does the regulating.

Gigaton

One billion tons. A ton is 2000 pounds so a gigaton is 2 trillion pounds!

Global Warming

A gradual increase in the overall temperature of the earth's atmosphere generally attributed to the greenhouse effect caused by increased levels of carbon dioxide, methane, chlorofluorocarbons and other pollutants. How global warming is experienced throughout the world depends on the area affected, where extreme weather events can range from increased precipitation and flooding, alternating patterns of drought and floods, drought-like and desert conditions. In a phenomenon known as subsidence land can sink as a result of, for example, the removal of groundwater from aquifers during time of drought, or even though it springs when ice sheets above it melt it still is less than the level of sea rise.

The Great Climate Diaspora

Another term coined by Joaquin that refers to the anticipated human migration from areas predominantly south to north due to increasing drought in the southern hemisphere of our planet.

Green Economy

An economy that "aims to reduce environmental risks and ecological scarcities and aims for sustainable development without degrading the environment."[147]

Greenhouse Effect _____

Most of the sun's radiant energy is the visible and near infrared spectrum. The air, when free of clouds and dust, is as transparent to this radiation as is the glass of a greenhouse.

Surfaces on the earth, or within the greenhouse, are warmed by sunlight and some of this warmth is transferred to the air from the surfaces in contact with the air. The warm air stays in the greenhouse mainly because the walls and glass roof prevent the restless wind from dissipating it. The earth is kept warm in a similar but not identical way. The earth absorbs the radiant heat emitted or coming from warm surfaces such as gases of carbon dioxide, water vapor and methane. These gases, which are present in the air although transparent to light, remain partially opaque to the longer wavelengths emitted by a warm surface.

The greenhouse effect has long kept the surface air warm and, in the absence of pollution, is benign. In fact, without it the earth would be 58° colder and probably incompatible with life.[148]

Greenhouse Gas _____

See greenhouse effect. Carbon dioxide (or CO_2), methane, soot and the other pollutants that we release into the atmosphere act like a blanket by trapping the sun's heat and warming the planet. This trapping mechanisms is likened to the construction of a greenhouse – a glass or transparent structure that when sunlight hits will keep and increase that heat inside as needed by certain plants especially.

Hardening Infrastructure _____

Not unlike security for computers, "hardening" implies security against weather events through either natural sources like berms, reefs and mangroves or man-made devices like seawalls, barriers and flood gates. Other ways include "dry flood-proofing" where buildings are made "as watertight as possible through the use of impermeable materials and flood barriers" while "wet flood-proofing" them allows "floodwaters to pass through [their] parking, storage, access or crawl spaces . . . without endangering structural stability."[149]

Hundred Year Flood Zone (100-year Flood Zone) _____

"An area with a 1 percent chance of flooding in any given year – not an area that will flood only once in a century. Several 100-year floods may follow one another in rapid succession."[150]

Ice Sheets _____

See effect of the melting of the polar ice caps; melting of the polar ice caps. An ice sheet – also known as a continental glac-ier – is a "glacier ice that covers the land surrounding it and is greater than 50,000 kilometers (20,000 miles) wide."[151] Antarc-tica in the South Pole, has about 90% of the world's ice . . . . about 7,000 feet thick . . . . about the size of the U.S.A. and Mexico";[152] in addition to the North Pole just over the Arctic Ocean and the Greenland ice sheet.

Ice sheets are different from ice caps and polar ice caps. Ice caps "cover less than 50,000 square kilometers and usually feed a series of glaciers around its edges. . . .and lie on top of moun-tains. . . . Polar ice caps are high-latitude regions covered in ice and are not strictly an ice cap (because they are usually larger than the 50,000 square km limit used to define ice caps) . . . [still] most people refer to these areas as ice caps anyway."[153]

Infrastructure

The basic physical and organizational structures and facilities (e.g., buildings, roads and power supplies) needed for the operation of a society or enterprise.

Investment Subsidies

A subsidy is a benefit given by the government to groups or individuals, usually in the form of a cash payment or a tax reduction. The subsidy is typically given to remove some type of burden in promotion of a public interest.[154]

Investment Tax Credit

An amount that businesses are allowed by law to deduct from their taxes that reflects an amount they reinvest in themselves. Lawmakers utilize this incentive to promote a larger economic policy of rewarding and encouraging economic growth.[155]

LEED Certification

LEED (Leadership in Energy and Environmental Design) is an ecology-oriented building certification program run under the auspices of the U.S. Green Building Council. LEED concentrates its efforts on improving performance across five key areas of environmental and human health: energy efficiency, indoor environmental quality, materials selection, sustainable site development and water savings.[156]

Levees _____

Traditional levees (also called dikes) are shaped like banks or hills (earthen embankments) located at the shoreline along riverbanks and along the ocean to direct the flow of water and protect communities from flooding. There are various types of levees including ones where concrete floodwalls are built on top of levees as surge barriers; and ring levees that encircle or go around an area as is found in the Midwest.

Life _____

Life exists simultaneously but separately in the realms of physics, chemistry and biology, and consequently has no decent scientific definition.

Physicists might define it as something that exists within bounds that spontaneously reduces it to entropy (disorder) while excreting disorder to the environment. Chemists would say that it is composed of macromolecules coming mainly from the elements of carbon, nitrogen, oxygen, hydrogen and, lesser but required proportions of, sulphur, phosphorous and iron, together with a suite of trace elements that includes selenium, iodine, cobalt and others.

Biochemists and physiologists would see life as always existing within cellular boundaries that hold an aqueous environment with a tightly regulated composition of ionic species including the elements sodium, potassium, calcium, magnesium and chlorine. Each of the cells carries a complete specification and instruction set written as a code on long, linear molecules of deoxyribonucleic acids (DNA). Biologists would define it as a dynamic state of matter that can replicate itself; the individual components will evolve by natural selection. Life can be observed, dissected and analyzed but it is an emergent phenomenon and may never be capable of rational expression.[157]

Managed Retreat

In the context of coastal erosion, managed retreat (also managed realignment) allows an area that was not previously exposed to flooding by the sea to become flooded by removing coastal protection. This process is usually in low-lying estuarine areas and, almost always, involves flooding of land, which may have at some point in the past been claimed by us from the sea.

In the UK, managed retreat is often a response to sea level rise exacerbated by local subsidence (caving in or sinking) of the land surface due to post-glacial isostatic rebound in the north.[158]

Melting of the Polar Ice Caps

See effect of the melting of the polar ice caps.

Methane

See melting of the polar ice caps. This colorless, odorless, flammable gas, CH_4, is the main by-product of the decomposition of organic matter by anaerobic bacteria (also known as marsh gas) as well as released from coal when it is mined. It is also the first member of the methane or alkane series of hydrocarbons.[159] The melting of the polar ice caps emits methane, a gas that is more threatening than carbon dioxide in terms of global warming. Its increase, measured in parts per billion, was 11 ppb from 2014 to 2015. This one-year increase almost doubled that from 2007 – 2013.[160]

Multiplier Effect _____

An effect in economics in which an increase in spending produces an increase in national income and consumption greater
than the initial amount spent. For example, if a corporation
builds a factory, it will employ construction workers and their
suppliers as well as those who work in the factory. Indirectly,
the new factory will stimulate employment in laundries, restau-
rants and service industries in the factory's vicinity.[161]

Multi-Purpose Levees _____

These types of levees perform functions in addition to protecting against flooding and storm surges. Depending on how the
raised bank, embankment, is configured it can also accommodate and "combine transit, highways, buildings, or parks either
on top or within the levee structure."[162]

Non-Renewable Energy / Non-Renewable Sources / Non-Renewables _____

Energy sources are classified as nonrenewable if they cannot be
replenished in a short period of time. Renewable energy
sources such as solar and wind can be replenished naturally in a
short period of time. There are four major nonrenewable energy sources: crude oil, natural gas, coal and uranium (natural
energy).

Nonrenewable energy sources come out of the ground as liquids, gases and solids. Crude oil (petroleum) is the only commercial nonrenewable fuel that comes naturally in liquid form.
Crude oil is used to make liquid petroleum products like gaso-

line, diesel fuel and heating oil. Propane and other gases such as butane and ethane are found in natural gas and crude oil. They are extracted and stored as liquids and are called liquid petroleum gases.

All fossil fuels are nonrenewable, but not all nonrenewable energy sources are fossil fuels. Coal, crude oil and natural gas are all considered fossil fuels because they were formed from the buried remains of plants and animals that lived millions of years ago.

Uranium ore, a solid, is mined and converted to a fuel used at nuclear power plants. Uranium is not a fossil fuel, but it is classified as a nonrenewable fuel.[163]

Paris Agreement _____

See COP21.

Parts per Million (PPM) _____

A unit used in science and engineering to measure very small values where there are no associated units of measurements. According to many climate experts, 350 parts per million or 350 ppm is considered a safe level for the amount of carbon dioxide in the atmosphere. It is now recorded globally that CO_2 levels globally have exceeded 400 ppm.[164]

Parts per Billion (PPM) _____

A unit used in science and engineering to measure extremely small values as with methane.

Positive and Negative Feedback __

See climate feedbacks. Self-regulating systems of any kind, from a simple thermostat-controlled cooker to you yourself, always include something that senses any departure from the desired or chosen state, a supply of energy and the means to apply force that opposes or encourages the deviation.

When a car we are driving deviates from out intended path we sense the deviation and, with our arms, we apply enough force to the steering wheel to turn the car's front wheels back on track. This is negative feedback. If by accident the steering mechanism were faulty, so that turning the steering wheel turned the front wheels so as to increase the deviation, this would be positive feedback. This is often a recipe for disaster, but positive feedback can be essential to make a system lively and rapidly responsive. When we talk of vicious circles, we are generally talking about positive feedback or actions we take that move us further in the same unhealthy direction.

Positive feedback is accelerating the direction that climate change is making, that is the warming temperatures, the melting of polar ice caps and the rising sea level.[165]

Public, Private and Community Partnerships (PuPCos) _____

A concept developed by Joaquin that calls for the development of a three-sector partnership framework consisting of the public, private and community sectors. In this partnership, the private sector would provide capital, technical capacity and development expertise. The public sector would provide "entitlements" in the form of financial incentives and subsidies as well as enhanced development rights and other zoning relief.

The inclusion of the community recognizes its role as oftentimes the end-user, capable of driving demand for the goods, services and amenities being offered and determining the success of the investment and development projects. This framework also recognizes that among the policy motivations for governments providing public entitlements is to benefit the public good in ways that include providing the community with employment and workforce development opportunities and the like. The inclusion and express acknowledgement of the community distinguishes PuPCos from more conventional PPPs or public-private partnerships.

Renewable Energy / Renewable Sources / Renewables

Any naturally occurring, theoretically inexhaustible source of energy, as biomass, solar, wind, tidal, wave and hydroelectric power that is not derived from fossil or nuclear fuel.[166]

Resilience (Adaptation)

Resilience / climate resilience / adaptation can be generally defined as the capacity for a socio-ecological system to: (1) absorb stresses and maintain function in the face of external stresses imposed upon it by climate change, and (2) adapt, reorganize and evolve into more desirable configurations that improve the sustainability of the system, leaving it better prepared for future climate change impacts.[167]

Resource Capitalism

A concept Eric developed that reflects the transition from an unsustainable state of finance capitalism oriented towards primarily money to a system that reflects the environmental and social impact of our activities in addition to economic ones. Resource capitalism provides a framework for combining the triple bottom line and the green economy, which as a system would reward responsible, sustainable use of resources and promote job growth and long-term economic development. In this way, Eric highlights the vast opportunities for new jobs, economic growth, innovation, local manufacturing and entrepreneurialism that exist with the adoption of a green economy.

Rolling Easements _____

See managed retreat. There are non-voluntary strategies for climate retreat, ranging from the extreme (e.g. eminent domain) to the more incremental and realistic, like rolling easements.

Rolling easements allow public control of land along the coast to migrate inland as beaches erode naturally or due to sea level rise, or a combination of both. Rolling easements prevent the construction of coastal armoring like sea walls and require that the permanent structures within the migrating easement be removed. This strategy ensures the migration of coastal ecosystems as the shoreline changes, as well as providing property owners with time to adjust to new conditions and plan accordingly. Texas is one of the states where rolling easements have been successfully legally challenged. As such their potential for widespread adoption remains unclear despite popularity with climate and urban planning experts.[168]

S + R Paradigm _____

We developed this concept in which sustainability (S) combined with resilience (R) incorporate a financing mechanism while providing a better overall integrated approach to infrastructure protection. The energy savings from sustainable measures can be used to finance physical improvements oriented around making the built environment more resilient towards weather events. James-Robert, along with Richard Kusack at The NRF and Built Environment, have been advising property owners and developers on making their large-scale buildings more resilient.

Sea Level

See effect of the melting polar ice caps. Imagine that you have a cup of water and you place a large rock in the middle; the water is the ocean and the rock is a continent. If you place an ice cube on top of the rock, eventually it will melt into the "ocean" around the rock, forcing water higher up around it. The same thing happens when polar ice caps melt. They melt directly into the ocean. In this way such melting increases the volume of water and force seas higher onto land.

As mentioned above with the effect of the melting of the polar ice caps an increase in the fresh water of the ice caps to water in the oceans decreases its salinity, or salt content.

Sea Level Rise / SLR

The so-called greenhouse effect or global warming may cause a sea level rise, which will have a great impact on the long-term movement and characteristics of the coast (more technically called coastal morphology). For example, the possible and gradual sea level rise will cause a general shoreline retreat as well as an increase in risk of flooding risk.[169]

Storm Water Management

See swales. Localized flooding can occur because a particular system when it combines storm water and sewage is overwhelmed by too much rain, melting snow or ice washes. Sewage systems in many older urban cities like New York are combined ones handling "both storm water and sewage on its way to treatment plants." Combined systems when inundated "lead to overflows and the discharge of sewage and pollutants into surrounding waterways." Design and engineering storm water management strategies include constructing "permeable paving, swales and dry wells [that] can temporarily capture runoff and reduce combined sewer overflows."[170]

Stranded Assets

A financial term that describes something that has become obsolete or nonperforming well ahead of its useful life, and must be recorded on a company's balance sheet as a loss of profit.[171]

Subsidence

Generally, this refers to land sinking as a result of, for example, the removal of groundwater from aquifers during time of drought, surface drainage for urban development and certain extraction processes of oil, natural gas and coal. Subsidence also refers to the relationship between the rising sea level and the eroding coastal land in Maine, New Hampshire and Massachusetts.[172]

In addition, "cracks in the earth caused by prolonged dry spells, as recently seen in parts of Europe, can tear apart the foundations of houses, bridges, factories and other structures, or cause whole buildings to collapse."[173]

Sunk Costs

In economics and business decision-making, a sunk cost is a cost that has already been incurred and cannot be recov-

ered. Sunk costs (also known as retrospective costs) are some-
times contrasted with prospective costs, which are future costs that may be incurred or changed if an action is
taken.[174]

Sustainability (Mitigation)

The quality of not being harmful to the environment or depleting natural resources and thereby supporting long-term ecological balance.[175]

Swales

Areas with soil or absorbent material, like a "bed of gravel, that
are designed to trap storm water runoff and hold it until it can
be safely emptied into a municipal storm sewer or into the
soil." "Landscaped strips of plantings along sidewalks or the
edges of buildings" are known as bioswales.[176]

Temperature

See effect of the melting polar ice caps. It is very important
that the polar ice caps are frozen because the snow they are
covered with reflects a large amount of light back into space
that would otherwise increase the overall temperature of earth.
The polar ice caps help keep the overall earth at a tolerable
temperature, but the melting of polar ice caps increases the rate
of global warming.

Threat Multipliers

The 2014 Quadrennial Defense Review, issued by the U.S. Department of Defense, succinctly describes climate change as a
"threat multiplier," in that climate change may exacerbate or

lead to other threats to security. Despite this recognition by the U.S. military, risk assessments that examine global, regional, national and subnational risks often fail to capture the "multiplier" effect of climate change. The climate change phenomenon is often either treated as an "environmental" factor, with little to no connection to other risk factors in the socio-political, economic and security spheres, or in some cases, as in the Fragile States Index (formerly the Failed State Index), not directly addressed.[177]

Tipping Point _____

See climate feedbacks; positive and negative feedback. Positive feedbacks when forcing or pushing a change in the direction it is going can be "a small change [having] large, long-term consequences for a system." Timothy Lenton lists various positive feedbacks that can serve as a tipping point such as permafrost melting and collapse; increasing absorption of solar radiation that is heating and melting the bottom of the sea ice; atmospheric circulation bringing warm air and warm ocean currents from the Atlantic into the Arctic; continued melting at the margins of the Greenland Ice Sheet; and warming ocean waters and longer snow-free seasons.[178]

APPENDIX A
HISTORIC PARIS AGREEMENT ON CLIMATE CHANGE

The following is excerpted from "Historic Paris Agreement on Climate Change." [179]

195 Nations Set Path to Keep Temperature Rise Well Below 2° Celsius

Paris, 12 December 2015 - An historic agreement to combat climate change and unleash actions and investment towards a low carbon, resilient and sustainable future was agreed by 195 nations in Paris today.

The Paris Agreement brings all nations into a common cause based on their historic, current and future responsibilities.

The universal agreement's main aim is to keep a global temperature rise this century well below 2 degrees Celsius and to drive efforts to limit the temperature increase even further to 1.5 degrees Celsius above pre-industrial levels.

The 1.5 degree Celsius limit is a significantly safer defense line against the worst impacts of a changing climate.

Additionally, the agreement aims to strengthen the ability to deal with the impacts of climate change.

To reach these ambitious and important goals, appropriate financial flows will be put in place, thus making stronger action by developing countries and the most vulnerable possible, in line with their own national objectives.

"The Paris Agreement allows each delegation and group of countries to go back home with their heads held high. Our collective effort is worth more than the sum of our individual effort. Our responsibility to history is immense" said Laurent Fabius, President of the COP 21 UN Climate change conference and French Foreign Minister.

The minister, his emotion showing as delegates started to rise to their feet, brought the final gavel down on the agreement to open and sustained acclamation across the plenary hall.

French President Francois Hollande told the assembled delegates: "You've done it, reached an ambitious agreement, a binding agreement, a universal agreement. Never will I be able to express more gratitude to a conference. You can be proud to stand before your children and grandchildren."

UN Secretary General Ban Ki-moon said: "We have entered a new era of global cooperation on one of the most complex issues ever to confront humanity. For the first time, every country in the world has pledged to curb emissions, strengthen resilience and join in common cause to take common climate action. This is a resounding success for multilateralism."

Christiana Figueres, Executive Secretary of the UN Framework Convention on Climate Change (UNFCCC), said: "One planet, one chance to get it right and we did it in Paris. We have made history together. It is an agreement of conviction. It is an agreement of solidarity with the most vulnerable. It is an agreement of long-term vision, for we have to turn this agreement into an engine of safe growth."

"Successive generations will, I am sure, mark the 12 December 2015 as a date when cooperation, vision, responsibility, a shared humanity and a care for our world took centre stage," she said.

"I would like to acknowledge the determination, diplomacy and effort that the Government of France have injected into this remarkable moment and the governments that have supported our shared ambition since COP 17 in Durban, South Africa," she said.

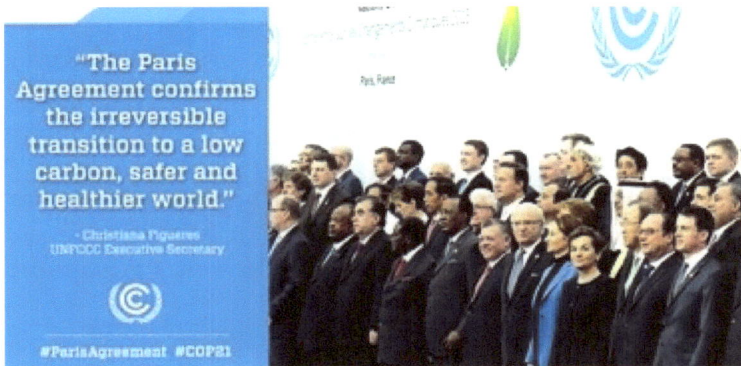

"The Paris Agreement confirms the irreversible transition to a low carbon, safer and healthier world."

- Christiana Figueres
UNFCCC Executive Secretary

#ParisAgreement #COP21

. . . ESSENTIAL ELEMENTS

The Paris Agreement and the outcomes of the UN climate conference (COP21) cover all the crucial areas identified as essential for a landmark conclusion:

o   Mitigation – reducing emissions fast enough to achieve the temperature goal

o   A transparency system and global stock-take – accounting for climate action

o   Adaptation – strengthening ability of countries to deal with climate impacts

o   Loss and damage – strengthening ability to recover from climate impacts
o   Support – including finance, for nations to build clean, resilient futures

As well as setting a long-term direction, countries will peak their emissions as soon as possible and continue to submit national climate action plans that detail their future objectives to address climate change.

This builds on the momentum of the unprecedented effort which has so far seen 188 countries contribute climate action plans to the new agreement, which will dramatically slow the pace of global greenhouse gas emissions.

The new agreement also establishes the principle that future national plans will be no less ambitious than existing ones, which means these 188 climate action plans provide a firm floor and foundation for higher ambition.

Countries will submit updated climate plans – called nationally determined contributions (NDCs) – every five years, thereby steadily increasing their ambition in the long-term.

Climate action will also be taken forward in the period before 2020. Countries will continue to engage in a process on mitigation opportunities and will put added focus on adaptation opportunities. Additionally, they will work to define a clear roadmap on ratcheting up climate finance to USD 100 billion by 2020

This is further underlined by the agreement's robust transparency and accounting system, which will provide clarity on countries' implementation efforts, with flexibility for countries' differing capabilities.

"The Paris Agreement also sends a powerful signal to the many thousands of cities, regions, businesses and citizens across the world already committed to climate action that their vision of a low-carbon, resilient future is now the chosen course for humanity this century," said Ms Figueres.

. . . SUPPORT TO DEVELOPING COUNTRIES

The Paris Agreement underwrites adequate support to developing nations and establishes a global goal to significantly strengthen adaptation to climate change through support and international cooperation.

The already broad and ambitious efforts of developing countries to build their own clean, climate-resilient futures will be supported by scaled-up finance from developed countries and voluntary contributions from other countries.

Governments decided that they will work to define a clear roadmap on ratcheting up climate finance to USD 100 billion by 2020 while also before 2025 setting a new goal on the provision of finance from the USD 100 billion floor.

Ms. Figueres said. "We have seen unparalleled announcements of financial support for both mitigation and adaptation from a multitude of sources both before and during the COP. Under the Paris Agreement, the provision of finance from multiple sources will clearly be taken to a new level, which is of critical importance to the most vulnerable."

International cooperation on climate-safe technologies and building capacity in the developing world to address climate change are also significantly strengthened under the new agreement.

SIGNING THE PARIS AGREEMENT

Following the adoption of the Paris Agreement by the COP (Conference of the Parties), it will be deposited at the UN in New York and be opened for one year for signature on 22 April 2016--Mother Earth Day.

The agreement will enter into force after 55 countries that account for at least 55% of global emissions have deposited their instruments of ratification.

CITIES AND PROVINCES TO COMPANIES AND INVESTORS ALIGNING

Today's landmark agreement was reached against the backdrop of a remarkable groundswell of climate action by cities and regions, business and civil society.

During the week of events under the Lima to Paris Action Agenda (LPAA) at the COP, the groundswell of action by these stakeholders successfully demonstrated the powerful and irreversible course of existing climate action.

Countries at COP 21 recognised the enormous importance of these initiatives, calling for the continuation and scaling up of these actions, which are entered on the UN-hosted NAZCA portal as an essential part in the rapid implementation of the Paris Agreement.

The scale of the Action Agenda globally is unprecedented, part of which is captured through Nazca and the LPAA:

o   Over 7,000 cities, including the most vulnerable to climate change, from over 100 countries with a combined population with one and a quarter billion people and around 32% of global GDP.

o   Sub-national states and regions comprising one fifth of total global land area and combined GDP of $12.5 trillion.

o   Over 5,000 companies from more than 90 countries who together represent the majority of global market capitalisation and over $38 trillion in revenue.

o   Nearly 500 investors with total assets under management of over $25 trillion

Christiana Figueres said: "The recognition of actions by businesses, investors, cities and regions is one of the key outcomes of COP 21. Together with the LPAA, the groundswell of action shows that the world is on an inevitable path toward a properly sustainable, low-carbon world."

MORE DETAILS . . .

o   All countries will submit adaptation communications, in which they may detail their adaptation priorities, support needs and plans. Developing countries will receive increased support for adaptation actions and the adequacy of this support will be assessed.

o   The existing Warsaw International Mechanism on Loss and Damage will be significantly strengthened.

o   The agreement includes a robust transparency framework for both action and support. The framework will provide clarity on countries' mitigation and adaptation actions, as well as the provision of support. At the same time, it recognizes that Least Developed Countries and Small Island Developing States have special circumstances.

o   The agreement includes a global stocktake starting in 2023 to assess the collective progress towards the goals of the agreement. The stocktake will be done every five years.

o The agreement includes a compliance mechanism, overseen by a committee of experts that operates in a non-punitive way.

The COP also closed on a number of technical issues.

o Under the Kyoto Protocol, there is now a clear and transparent accounting method for carry-over credits for the second commitment period, creating a clear set of rules.

o The first round of international assessment and review process (IAR) that was launched in 2014 was successfully completed.

o A number of technical and implementation issues related to the existing arrangements on technology, adaptation, action for climate empowerment and capacity building were also successfully concluded.

UNFCCC

With 196 Parties, the United Nations Framework Convention on Climate Change (UNFCCC) has near universal member-protocol has been ratified by 192 of the UNFCCC Parties. For the first commitment period of the Kyoto Protocol, 37 States, consisting of highly industrialized countries and countries undergoing the process of transition to a market economy, have legally binding emission limitation and reduction commitments. In Doha in 2012, the Conference of the Parties serving as the meeting of the Parties to the Kyoto Protocol adopted an amendment to the Kyoto

Protocol, which establishes the second commitment period under the Protocol. The ultimate objective of both treaties is to stabilize greenhouse gas concentrations in the atmosphere at a level that will prevent dangerous human interference with the climate system.

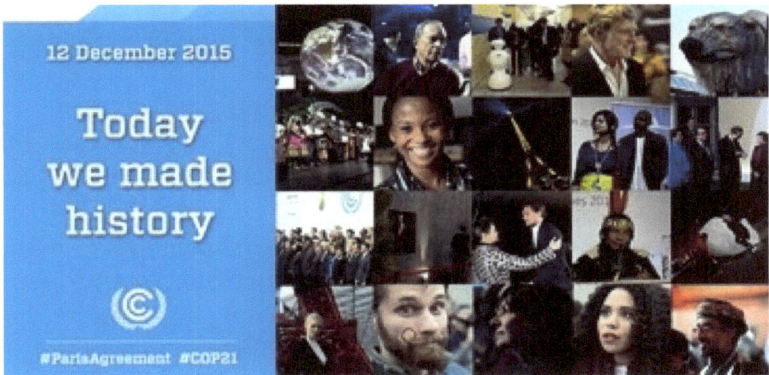

12 December 2015

Today we made history

#ParisAgreement #COP21

APPENDIX B
THE NATURAL RESILIENCE FOUNDATION

SUMMARY OF WHITE PAPER

o The NRF is a development stage company.

o The NRF intends to provide first loss subsidies for multi-family and commercial property sustainability and resilience retrofits.

o The NRF will ideally be able to finance 100% of the cost of sustainability/resilience retrofits so property owners and businesses will not be out-of-pocket.

o The NRF requires a $500,000 working capital fund to do studies, commence marketing efforts and fund the first year of operations.

o The proposed Climate Resilience Investment Subsidy Fund (CRIS) is $100M-$250M. It is anticipated that property and casualty insurers, utility companies and municipalities will finance this fund.

o The ten (10) Protect, Enhance & Preserve (PEP) Measures:

1) Expand Sustainable/Resilient Communities through the development of a master resilience plan (see PlaNYC report of June 2013 for useful guidelines).
http://www.nyc.gov/html/sirr/html/report/report.shtml

2)   Promote and broaden flood accommodative design and engineering to be accomplished in conjunction with public & private resilience efforts.

3)   Encourage efficient storm water management through deployment of portable flood barriers, mold resistant foam insulation and wallboard, climate resilient landscaping, installation of permeable surfaces and additions to property elevations above flood levels.

4)   Promote use of clean energy through implementation of passive and renewable technologies.

5)   Utilize cutting edge high efficiency heating, cooling and ventilation technologies.

6)   Improve building envelope to achieve optimum balance of air flow reducing loss of heat flow in the winter and cool air in the summer.

7)   Connect natural world elements with internal property improvements such that streetscapes and public areas, which in turn, protect and align with private property investment, improve flood prone areas.

8)   Relocate building infrastructure above projected flood levels (including reasonable projections for sea level rise over a 50-year useful life assumption).

9)   Create resilient and sustainable connectivity between utility grid and individual properties.

10)   Utilize earth friendly building materials. Encourage reuse, recycling and renewal policies in building program with a focus on the use of zero VOC materials.

FOUNDERS / BOARD MEMBERS BIOGRAPHIES

Eric Kaufman, author of **A Call to Action: How to Save Millions of Lives**, has over 33 years of real estate experience as a broker, investor, contractor and developer of commercial (office, retail, hotel, industrial, multi-family) real estate valued at about $1 billion.   During the 80's, through Creative Capital Group, which he established with his mother, Joan Kaufman, he saw the conversion of 1,100 apartments in New York and New Jersey into co-operatives and condominiums. He then joined in the 90s, The Carlton Group – a real estate banking firm – as Senior Managing Director.

In 2008, he began developing with Meir Laufer the concept of a giant Ferris wheel in New York City modeled after the London Eye. The New York Wheel, under a public-private partnership with the City of New York, as of November 2016 is half constructed and capitalized with $610 million of private money. In April 2018 the New York Wheel is scheduled to open in Staten Island, NYC.

During the Internet's early days, Kaufman also launched *WorldWide Network Magazine* as a B2B and a B2C link. By 1992, he incorporated in the magazine a computer bulletin board known as Global Electronic Marketplace (GEM), which was the forerunner of Google, AOL and eBay. Kaufman learned how important it is to "time the market" with innovative concepts.

Kaufman learned of the concept of "climate resilience" in September 2012 during an American Institute of Architects event in Manhattan. Following Superstorm Sandy, he along with Ellie Sugarman, Joaquin Matias and James-Robert Sellinger, formed The Natural Resilience Foundation as a 501(c) (3) public charity in August 2013 to advocate and develop financing strategies to safeguard life, real estate and critical infrastructure from the effects of extreme weather patterns.

Kaufman has an A.B. in Psychology from Vassar College and an MBA from the Wharton School, with a Marketing concentration and a minor in Finance. He now resides in Austin, Texas.

Joaquin F. Matias, co-author and editor of **A Call to Action: How to Save Millions of Lives**, is an attorney, public management executive and business entrepreneur experienced in government, higher education and non-profit, private and entrepreneurial sectors. He is committed to advancing urban economic development, social entrepreneurship, good governance and sustainable and resilient communities.

As a Co-Founder and Board Member of The Natural Resilience Foundation, Matias formulated many of its policies and key documents. He is also a Partner at City Strategy Group, LLC, where as the Chief Strategy Officer, he is developing initiatives that promote innovation and public / private initiatives to rebuild urban communities and cities into desirable sustainable and resilient locations.

Matias has held senior level positions in the government, non-profit and for profit sectors. As Director of Economic Development for the City of Newark, he negotiated and managed many complex, multi-phase, large-scale commercial, industrial, retail, retail/residential mixed-use and sports developments. As Executive Director of Real Estate & Economic Development for Rutgers University (Newark), Matias advanced the growth of the Newark campus of Rutgers around public-private partnerships, multi-use and shared facilities, and value-added research and civic engagement.

At the Rutgers School of Public Affairs and Administration, Matias also developed and taught a graduate seminar course entitled "Redefining Economic Development from an Urban

Perspective: Turning Collapse into Opportunity." He is a former Ford Foundation Fellow, during which he authored an article – "From Work Units to Corporations: Chinese Corporate Governance in a Transitional Market Economy" – that was published in the New York International Law Review (Winter 1998).

Matias is a member of the New York Bar with an A.B. and M.P.A. from Harvard University and J.D. from Northeastern University.

James-Robert Sellinger is a Co-founder and Board Member of The Natural Resilience Foundation. He is a real estate executive with over 25 years' experience in diverse institutional and entrepreneurial environments. Sellinger has a successful career in transactional commercial real estate and a record of formulating creative financial structures within the capital, property and asset markets.

Sellinger is also involved in funding a ground up land development for senior housing properties as a principal of SLD. As former Chairman of the Tenafly (NJ) Planning Board, he was instrumental in advocating its Green Agenda and sustainability and resilience efforts to alleviate storm water runoff.

His past positions have included Manager and Senior Underwriter at Merrill Lynch Mortgage Capital, Senior Director at the hedge fund Palisades Financial, Mortgage Banker at Northmarq Capital, and Manager with AT&T Real Estate.

Sellinger has a B.B.A from University of MA, Amherst and an M.B.A. from Cornell University. He is currently an Adjunct Professor in the graduate program at the Schack Real Estate Institute, New York University.

Ellie Sugarman is a Co-Founder and Board Member of The Natural Resilience Foundation. She is an alumna of The School of Environmental Science at the University of New Hampshire. Sugarman graduated Summa Cum Laude with a B.S. Ed from St. Thomas Aquinas College in Sparkill, N.Y. and Summa Cum Laude with a M.S. Ed from Western Connecticut State University. She also received her degree in Business Management as Valedictorian of her graduating class at Southern Vermont College.

Sugarman was influenced at a young age by the works of Rachel Carson, especially *Silent Spring*, and by Frances Moore Lappé's *Diet for a Small Planet*, as well as by her grandfather, who was early proponent of reusing and recycling natural resources. As a kindergarten teacher, she taught ecological sustainability to hundreds of young children. She was featured in a children's book by Katie Davis entitled, *Kindergarten Rocks!*

APPENDIX C
ELEVATION OF VARIOUS US CITIES

ALTITUDES OF MAJOR US CITIES[180]

This chart provides the altitude over various airports throughout the country, which may differ significantly from the altitude of downtown areas. We have highlighted in yellow areas with an altitude of less than 100 feet of elevation above sea level – as areas that would be vulnerable to the effects of sea level rise.

CITY BY STATE	AIRPORT	ELEVATION (FT)
ALABAMA		
Birmingham	Birmingham	644
Mobile	Bates Field	218
Montgomery	Dannelly Fld	221
ALASKA		
Anchorage	Anchorage Intl	144
Fairbanks	Fairbanks Intl	531
ARIZONA		
Grand Canyon	Grand Canyon N.P.	6606
Phoenix	Sky Harbor	1132
Tucson	Tucson Intl	2641
ARKANSAS		
Little Rock	Adams Field	258

CALIFORNIA		
Bakersfield	Meadows Field	507
Fresno	Fresno Air Term	332
Los Angeles	LAX	126
Mojave	Mojave	2787
Redding	Redding Municipal	502
Sacramento	Sacramento Metro	23
San Diego	Lindbergh	15
San Francisco	San Francisco Intl	11
COLORADO		
Colorado Springs	C.S. Municipal	6172
Denver	Centennial	5883
Grand Junction	Walker Field	4858
Gunnison	Gunnison County	7673
CONNECTICUT		
Hartford/Windsor	Bradley Intl	174
DELAWARE		
Wilmington	New Castle County	80
DISTRICT OF COLUMBIA		
Washington, D.C.	Reagan Intl	16
FLORIDA		
Jacksonville	Jax Intl	30
Miami	Miami Intl	11

Tallahassee	Talahassee Regional	81
GEORGIA		
Augusta	Bush Field	145
Atlanta	Hartsfield Intl	1026
Savannah	Savannah Intl	51
HAWAII		
Hilo	Hilo Intl	47
Honolulu	Honolulu Intl	13
IDAHO		
Boise	Boise Air Terminal	2858
Idaho Falls	Fanning Field	4740
Pocatello	Pocatello Muni	4449
ILLINOIS		
Champaign/Urbana	U of Illinois – Willard	754
Chicago	O'Hare Intl	668
Chicago - Rockford	Midway	619
Rockford	Greater Rockford	736
Springfield	Capital	597
INDIANA		
Fort Wayne	Baer Field	815
Indianapolis	Indianapolis Intl	797
IOWA		
Cedar Rapids	Cedar Rapids Intl	864
Des Moines	Des Moines Intl	957

KANSAS		
Hutchinson	Hutchinson Municpal	1542
Topeka	Forbes Field	1080
KENTUCKY		
Lexington	Bluegrass	980
LOUSIANA		
Lake Charles	Chennault	17
New Orleans	New Orleans Intl	4
MAINE		
Bangor	Bangor Intl	192
Portland	Portland Intl	74
MARYLAND		
Baltimore	BWI	146
MASSACHUSETTS		
Boston	Logan Intl	20
MICHIGAN		
Detroit	Wayne County	639
Grand Rapids	Kent County	794
Lansing	Capital City	861
MINNESOTA		
Duluth	Duluth/Superior Intl	1430
Minneapolis	Minneapolis/St. Paul	841

MISSISSIPPI		
Jackson	Jackson Intl	346
Meridian	Key Field	297
MISSOURI		
Kansas City	Kansas City Intl	1026
St. Louis	Lambert	605
MONTANA		
Billings	Billings/Logan	3649
Helena	Helena Regional	3873
NEBRASKA		
Grand Island	Central Nebraska Regional	1846
Lincoln	Lincoln Municipal	1214
Omaha	Eppley	983
NEVADA		
Las Vegas	McCarran Intl	2174
Reno	Cannon	4412
NEW HAMPSHIRE		
Manchester	Genier	234
NEW JERSEY		
Atlantic City	Atlantic City Intl	76
Newark	Newark Intl	18
NEW MEXICO		
Albuquerque	Albuquerque Intl	5352
Roswell	Roswell Industrial Air Center	3669
Santa Fe	Santa Fe Municipal	6344

NEW YORK		
Albany	Albany County	285
Buffalo	Greater Buffalo Intl	724
New York City	JFK	13
New York City	LaGuardia	20
Rochester	Greater Rochester Intl	559
Syracuse	Hancock	421
NORTH CAROLINA		
Asheville	Asheville Regional	2165
Raleigh	Raleigh/Durham	437
NORTH DAKOTA		
Bismarck	Bismarck Intl	1677
OHIO		
Akron	Akron/Canton Regional	1228
Cleveland	Hopkins Intl	792
Columbus	Port Columbus Intl	816
OKLAHOMA		
Oklahoma City	Will Rogers	1295
Tulsa	Tulsa Intl	677
OREGON		
Klamath Falls	Klamath Falls Intl	4092
Portland	Portland Intl	27
Redmond	Roberts Field	3077

PENNSYLVANIA		
Harrisburg	Harrisburg Intl	310
Philadelphia	Philadelphia Intl	21
Pittsburgh	Greater Pittsburgh Intl	1203
Wilkes Barre	W-B/Scranton Intl	962
RHODE ISLAND		
Providence	T F Green Intl	55
SOUTH CAROLINA		
Charleston	Charleston Intl	45
Columbia	Columbia Metro-politan	236
SOUTH DAKOTA		
Rapid City	Rapid City Regional	3202
TENNESSEE		
Memphis	Memphis Intl	332
TEXAS		
Austin	R. Mueller Municipal	632
Austin	Bergstom Intl	542
Dallas	DFW Intl	603
El Paso	El Paso Intl	3956
Houston	Houston Intl	98
San Antonio	San Antonio Intl	809
UTAH		
Ogden	Ogden/Hinckley	4470
Provo	Provo Municipal	4491
Salt Lake City	SLC Intl	4227

VERMONT		
Burlington	Burlington Intl	334
VIRGINIA		
Norfolk	Norfolk Intl	27
Richmond	Byrd Field	168
WASHINGTON		
Ephrata	Ephrata Municipal	1272
Seattle	Sea-Tac Intl	429
Spokane	Spokane Intl	2372
Yakima	Yakima Air Terminal	1095
WEST VIRGINIA		
Charleston	Yeager	982
Martinsburg	Shepherd	557
WISCONSIN		
Madison	Truax Field	862
Milwaukee	Mitchell	723
WYOMING		
Casper	Natrona County	5348
Rock Springs	Rock Springs Municipal	6760

APPENDIX D
IMAGES OF THE FOOD CHAIN

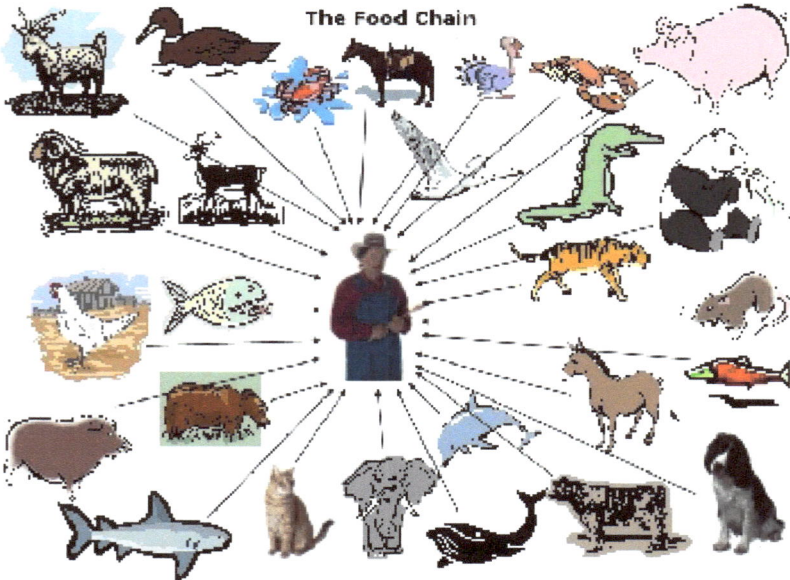

This Food Chain diagram shows "Man" at the center.
Source: Blog.chrisworfolk.com

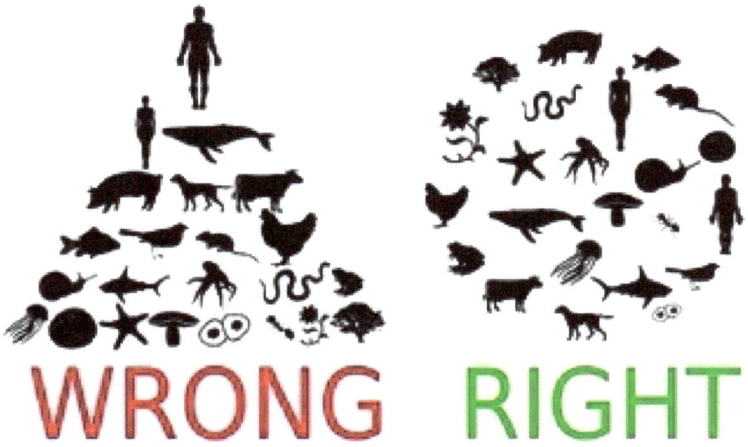

WRONG   RIGHT

On the left, the "man-centric" diagram has man at the top of a Food Chain pyramid. On the right, a holistic interdependent Food Chain organized as a circle. Source: chan4chan.com

APPENDIX E
CAPITAL BUDGETING / COST-BENEFIT ANALYSIS

We provide the following exercise as illustrating the type of Cost-Benefit Analysis we would undertake when evaluating potential Climate Resilience (Adaptation) Projects and determining the feasibility of establishing of Relocation Communities / Cities. In both situations, government analysts, legislators and officials should seek to understand and quantify, when possible, the costs incurred by residents, businesses and property owners as well as the burden imposed on government budgets and operations when remaining in existing low-lying, coastal, or drought-stricken areas made vulnerable to the effects of extreme weather events.

This type of exercise will demonstrate the need for capital budgets to be re-examined, adjusted and increased to reflect the future needs of a municipality facing the impact of extreme weather variability.

This valuable exercise is a "work in progress" that will be refined by practitioners engaged by municipalities to undertake this type of analysis.

Step 1	Add up the value of all existing properties – compartmentalized into private sector and public sector categories and property types. This number will give us the total value of the real property in the municipality.

Step 2   Add up the value of all public infrastructure in-cluding roads, bridges, waste and storm water treatment plants, water infrastructure and utility investments. This number will give us the total value of the public infrastructure for the munic-ipality.

Sum of Step 1 and Step 2

Represents the total value of the municipality's real property and public infrastructure at a par-ticular point in time, and, like a balance sheet, represents the total assets of the municipality at a particular point in time.

Step 3   Calculate the costs of all operations needed by the particular municipality such as and including public services like police, fire, water, education and other services that the municipality pro-vides for a particular area.

Step 4   Estimate the cost of the climate adaptation measures necessary to maintain the municipality along 10 / 20 / 50 / 100 year periods. Calcu-late the present value of these future costs by using the municipality's cost of capital.

Step 5   Estimate the projected future disaster-related expenditures due to storm surges, droughts, wildfires, etc. for the same 10 / 20 / 50 / 100 year periods. Calculate the present value of these future costs by using the municipality's cost of capital.

Even though the occurrence of future disasters remains uncertain, assumptions could be made at the 10 / 25 / 50 / 75 / 100 year periods. At this stage of analysis, a weighted average could suffice rather than a full-blown statistical analysis of the probability of a damaging storm at various year assumptions.

Step 6 Estimate the cost of relocating the affected segments / portions of the population to a less weather sensitive or a more climate resilient location including, for example, the costs of property buy-outs, relocation, infrastructure and the intangibles of social, psychological and political factors. Clearly quantifying the intangibles will be very difficult but certain proxies like costs of counseling and increased reliance on public benefits may be used.

The end of the analysis will result in a "relocation cost per person" to an elevated or less weather sensitive location.

Step 7 Segregate public costs from private costs and factor in the impact, if any, of federal, state or local grants, subsidies as well as insurance proceeds from future disasters that may apply to reduce the costs for Steps 4-6 so that these costs will be Net Costs calculated on a Net Present Value (again based on municipality's cost of capital).

Step 8	Determine the existing budget to serve as a baseline (baseline budget), that is all revenue sources including local tax revenue allocated to property and infrastructure maintenance and public services, capital reserves, property taxes, investment and bond proceeds, licenses, and state and federal aid. Based on this baseline budget prepare 10 / 20 / 50 / 100 year budgets where these budgets are increased by a reasonable and customary percentage for property taxes and the like.
Step 9	Analysts may also project <u>higher</u> future 10 / 20 / 50 / 100 year budgets by <u>first</u> changing the allocations currently made in the baseline budget <u>and</u> applying more aggressive increases in property taxes, licenses and revenue sources under the municipality's control.
Step 10	Analyze and compare (a) the cost of maintaining a particular municipality as calculated / estimated in Steps 3 to 7, <u>provided</u> all properties have a positive Net Present Value as determined in Steps 1 and 2 <u>and</u> (b) the budgets produced in Steps 8 and 9.
Conclusion	If during Step 10, the costs greatly exceed the budgets prepared in Steps 8 and 9, then municipality and its inhabitants may have to seriously consider relocation.

At the same time, this exercise may guide municipalities in starting now to adjust their capital budgets and prepare so that if their budgets are increased in line with Step 9 or the needs projected in Steps 3-7, relocation may not be required (as least from a financial perspective).

APPENDIX F
COUNTRIES IN THE PATH OF THE GREAT CLIMATE DIASPORA

Russia/Siberia
Latvia
Lithuania
Finland
Sweden
Norway
Denmark
Iceland
Ukraine
Greenland
Northern Canada/Quebec
Slovenia
Czechoslovakia
Poland
Romania
Hungary
Bulgaria
Georgia
Serbia
Austria

APPENDIX G
"HOW TO SAVE MILLION(S) OF LIVES" POWERPOINT DECK

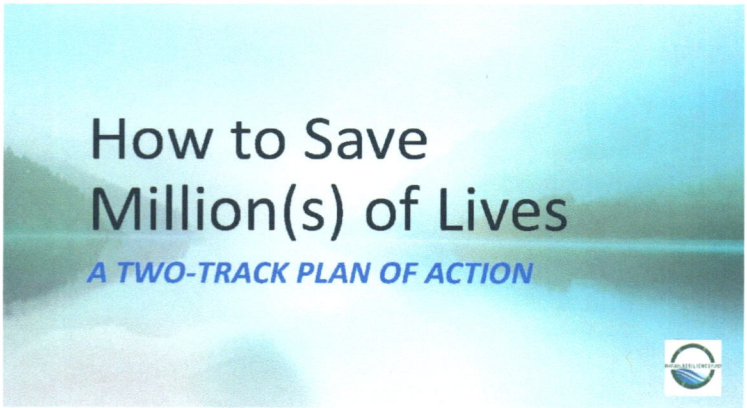

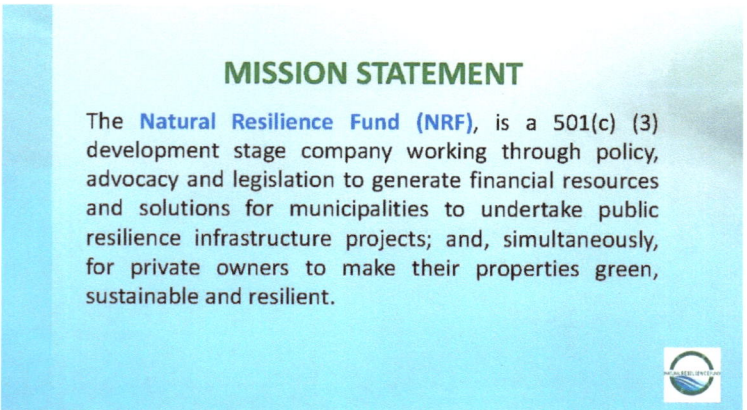

How to Save Million(s) of Lives
A TWO-TRACK PLAN OF ACTION

MISSION STATEMENT

The **Natural Resilience Fund (NRF)**, is a 501(c) (3) development stage company working through policy, advocacy and legislation to generate financial resources and solutions for municipalities to undertake public resilience infrastructure projects; and, simultaneously, for private owners to make their properties green, sustainable and resilient.

NRF'S APPROACH

- Link sustainability and resiliency under NRF's S+R©™ Approach so energy savings are re-invested into resiliency initiatives;
- Utilize a single protocol of 10 strategic, high-value actions to "protect, enhance and preserve" lives, properties and essential public services (PEP Measures©™);
- Advocate federal, state and local governments to provide Tax Credits and Subsidies allowing individuals and corporations to support resiliency projects as well as motivate landlords; and
- Prepare existing cities as well as create new Relocation Cities (R Cities) for the "Great Climate-Change Diaspora."

NRF'S ACCOMPLISHMENTS

- Finalist in the Adaptation Category of MIT's Climate Co-Lab Competition for NRF's concept of tax credits (CR-ITCs).
- Advocacy efforts led to NYC increasing its planning area for lower Manhattan's coast (a/k/a the "Dryline") from 1.8 miles to 5 miles.
- Advocacy efforts led to NYC increasing its planning dollars for the Dryline Area from $3M to $14M and contributing $100M of City money to leverage federal dollars.
- Working with developers to install "intermediate" green, friendly co-generation plants as well as advanced geo-thermal technology in collaboration with Dutch companies.
- Contributing to the emerging resiliency field with "out-of-box" proposals, government and international consultations.

SUSTAINABILITY + RESILIENCY

- Sustainability in the U.S. is about reducing energy use; "mitigation" is term preferred elsewhere.
- Resiliency in the U.S. is about mitigating the effects of extreme weather events / effects of climate change; "adaptation" is the term preferred elsewhere.
- S and R (or M and A) are complementary but separate concepts.
- NRF's S+R©™ paradigm (M+A) leverage the financial benefits of S to finance R.

TAX CREDITS

Tax credits can generate massive amounts of capital. Proceeds can jump-start "green" world economy, create millions of jobs, fund / provide subsidies for S+R projects launched on a large-scale.

NRF's Climate Resilience Investment Tax Credit (CR-ITC)©™ platform can help realize objectives of the Paris COP 21 Accord, December 2015.

TAX CREDITS

NRF's CR-ITC©™ platform envisions individuals and companies getting a dollar for dollar reduction in their income taxes for every dollar they contribute to a publicly approved resiliency / adaptation projects ("Eligible Projects").

What does this mean: Donate or contribute $100 to Eligible Projects and reduce your personal or company taxes by the same $100.

How would money be used: If 1.5% of the 9.5M NYC taxpayers each gave $500, $71M could be raised each year to
✓ finance large-scale resilience projects or
✓ float billion dollar bonds or
✓ generate the $100B owed to developing countries under the 2009 Copenhagen Accord for their climate adaptation (resilience) efforts scheduled to begin in 2020.

SUBSIDIES

NRF's Climate Resilience Investment Subsidies (CRIS)©™ would close the financing gap. Programs like Property Assessment Clean Energy (PACE) Financing provides most but not the financing generally related to resiliency measures.

Sources of Subsidies: NRF envisions raising these dollars for subsidies from
✓ proceeds generated from NRF's CR-ITC©™ platform; and
✓ from a fund created and paid into by insurance and utility companies.

GREAT CLIMATE CHANGE DIASPORA

Though we must continue efforts – like S+R, Tax Credits and Subsidies ("Plan B") – we cannot avoid the damage to be caused by on-going global warming and rising temperatures. Melting polar ice caps and glaciers, compounded by the release of methane, will accelerate and result in flooding of cities like London, Beijing, New York, Dhaka and Kolkata.

NRF wants to establish Plan Relocation ("Plan R") to prepare certain existing cities and build TODAY new "Relocation Cities" – ones that are sustainable and resilient as places for individuals/ families displaced and dislocated by climate change.

HUMAN BEINGS MUST PREPARE FOR THE INEVITABLE.
THE ANIMALS ARE ALREADY MIGRATING

The Biblical Diaspora

The Jewish Diaspora 500 BCE - 500 CE

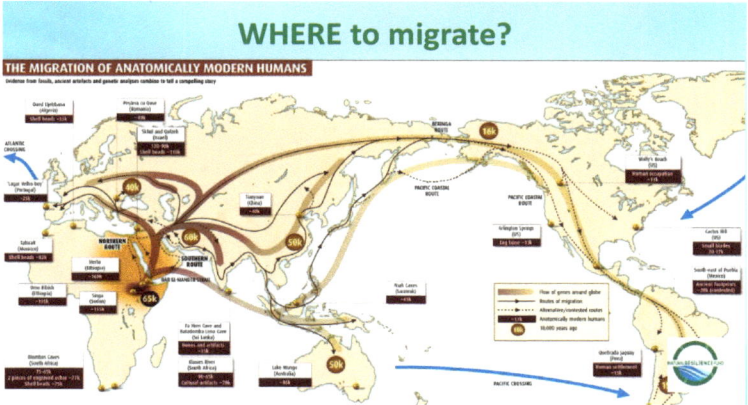

GREAT CLIMATE CHANGE DIASPORA

<u>Milestone 1</u>: Identify NOW cities and locations for new Relocation Cities on the basis of such factors such as
- ✓ Location on higher ground, less vulnerable to coastal flooding;
- ✓ Adequate supply of clean water and not vulnerable to drought;
- ✓ An existing infrastructure of public transportation;
- ✓ Supply of arable land to practice sustainable farming;
- ✓ Location within key areas of each continent / global community; and
- ✓ A readiness on the political, social and economic level for instituting consistent sustainable and resilient practices.

GREAT CLIMATE CHANGE DIASPORA

<u>Milestone 2</u>: Complete planning and design by 2030

- ✓ Identify existing usable infrastructure, resources;
- ✓ Design and plan hyperdensity according to NRF's PEP Measures;
- ✓ Select technologies

GREAT CLIMATE CHANGE DIASPORA

Milestone 3: Establish governance structures

Complete construction by 2040

Milestone 4: Migration flows 2040 - 2050

RISK ANALYSIS
Plan B AND PLAN R

- If Paris COP-21 has not shown positive results by 2020, accelerate Plan R (Relocation)
- Need massive amounts of public and private investment
- Need simultaneous political, public and business will.

	Plan B	Plan R
Risk 1	Timing	Timing
Risk 2	Uncertainty	Uncertainty
Risk 3	Must work with and not against nature	Must work with and not against nature

BLOG / EXPLORE / COMMENT

The NRF is a developmental stage entity interested in getting your comments on its concepts and designs. Dialog is the first step of a grass roots effort needed to start a global response to a critical matter of global concern. Your engagement is necessary to then trigger legislators to act. Comment on our blog:

http://natresilience.blogspot.com.

Also check out our website:

www.naturalresiliencefund.org.

We are also on Facebook, Linkedin, Instagram and Twitter.

DONATIONS

As a 501(c)(3) corporation, we appreciate any donations you can make to help defray the costs of making The NRF operational.

The Natural Resilience Fund, Inc.

APPENDIX H
MASLOW ON
SELF-ACTUALIZED PEOPLE

Although we are all, theoretically, capable of self-actualizing, most of us will not do so, or only to a limited degree. According to Abraham Maslow, self-actualization is about achieving one's potential and is not a judgment on their character or demeanor. He estimated that only two percent of people reach the state of self-actualization. All references in this section are from his works widely known, but you can review these basic components online.[181]

By studying 18 people he considered to be self-actualized (including Abraham Lincoln and Albert Einstein) Maslow identified 15 characteristics of a self-actualized person.

1. They perceive reality efficiently and can tolerate uncertainty;
2. They accept themselves and others for what they are;
3. They are spontaneous in thought and action;
4. They are problem-centered (not self-centered);
5. They have an unusual sense of humor;
6. They are able to look at life objectively;
7. They are highly creative;
8. They are resistant to enculturation, but not purposely unconventional;
9. They are concerned with the welfare of humanity;
10. They are capable of deep appreciation of basic life-experience;
11. They establish deep satisfying interpersonal relationships with a few people;

12.   They experience moments of pure joy and elation also known as peak experiences;
13.   They need privacy;
14.   They have democratic attitudes; and
15.   They have strong moral/ethical standards.

Maslow further identified behaviors that would lead to increasing self-actualization.

1.   Experiencing life like a child, with full absorption and concentration;
2.   Trying new things instead of sticking to safe paths;
3.   Listening to your own feelings in evaluating experiences instead of the voice of tradition, authority or the majority;
4.   Avoiding pretense or game playing and instead is honest;
5.   Being prepared to be unpopular if your views do not coincide with those of the majority;
6.   Taking responsibility and working hard; and
7.   Trying to identify your defenses and having the courage to give them up.

Individuals achieve self-actualization in their own unique way, but they tend to share certain of these characteristics and behaviors.   And while there are degrees of self-actualization, "there are no perfect human beings" or self-actualization be equated with perfection. Not all 15 characteristics are required to become self-actualized and not only self-actualized people will display them.

BIBLIOGRAPHY

Anthony, Sebastian. "Thorium nuclear reactor trial begins, could provide cleaner, safer, almost-waste-free energy." *Extreme Tech*, July 1, 2013. http://www.extremetech.com.

Brown, Lester R. *Plan B 3.0 – Mobilizing to Save Civilization.* Earth Policy Institute. New York: W.W. Norton & Company, 2008.

Brown, Lester R. *Plan B 4.0 – Mobilizing to Save Civilization.* Earth Policy Institute. New York: W.W. Norton & Company, 2009.

Burnett, John. "Billions Spent on Flood Barriers, but New Orleans still a 'Fishbowl.'" *NPR*, August 28, 2015. http://www.NPR.org.

Carson, Rachel. *Silent Spring.* Boston: Houghton Mifflin, 1962.

Chakrabarti, Vishaan. *A Country of Cities: A Manifesto for an Urban America.* Metropolis Books, 2013.

Colman, Zach. "East vs. West in coal mine battle." *Washington Examiner*, August 26, 2015. http://www.washingtonexaminer.com.

Diamond, Jared. *Collapse: How Societies Choose to Fail or Succeed.* London: Penguin Books, 2011.

Dyer, Gwynne. *Climate Wars: The Fight for Survival as the World Overheats.* Mass Market Paperback, 2011.

Endicot, Neil. "Thorium-Fuelled Molten Salt Reactors." *Weinberg Foundation*. http://www.the-weinberg-foundation.org.

Forero, Juan. "In Colombia newfound wealth masks poverty." *Washington Post*, February 1, 2009. http://www.archive.boston.com.

Freudenberg, Robert, Lucretia Montemayor Solano and Ellis Calvin. "Whitepaper - Where to Reinforce, Where to Retreat?" *Regional Planning Association*, May 22, 2015.

Fuller, Buckminster R. *The Dymaxion World of Buckminster Fuller*. New York: Anchor Press, Doubleday Company, 1960.

Fuller, Buckminster R. *Earth, Inc.* New York: Anchor Press, Doubleday & Company, 1973.

Fuller, Buckminster R. *Nine Chains to the Moon*. Philadelphia: J.B. Lippincott Company, 1938.

Fuller, Buckminster R. with E.J. Applewhite. *Synergetics: Explorations in the Geometry of Thinking*. New York: MacMillan Publishing Company, 1975.

Funk, Mackenzie. *Windfall: The Blooming Business of Global Warming.* New York: Penguin Press, 2014.

Gore, Al. *An Inconvenient Truth.* London: Bloomsbury, 2006.

Gore, Al. *The Future: Six Drivers of Global Change.* New York: Random House, 2013.

Houghton, Sir John. *Global Warming*. London: Cambridge University Press, 2004.

Howell, Elizabeth Howell. "How Long Have Humans Been On Earth." *Universe Today*, December 23, 2015.

Hunt, Heidi. "Homesteading and Livestock." *Mother Earth News*, July 13, 2007.

Kahn, Herman, William Brown and Leon Martel. *The Next 200 Years: A Scenario for America and the World.* New York: William Morrow, 1976.

Kaplan, Thomas. "Cuomo Seeking Home Buyouts in Flood Zone." *New York Times*, February 3, 2013.

Kolbert, Elizabeth. *The Sixth Extinction: An Unnatural History.* New York: MacMillan and Company, 2014.

Kurzweil, Ray. *The Age of Spiritual Machines: When Computers Exceed Human Intelligence.* New York: Viking, 1999.

Kurzweil, Ray. *How to Create Mind: The Secret of Human Thought Revealed.* New York: Viking, Penguin Group, 2012.

Kurzweil, Ray. *The Singularity is Near: When Humans Transcend Biology.* New York: Viking, 2006.

Lawson, Nigel. *An Appeal to Reason: A Cool Look at Global Warming.* London: Gerald Duckworth & Co. Ltd., 2008.

Lovelock, James. *The Ages of Gaia.* New York: W.W. Norton, 1988.

Lovelock, James. *Gaia: A New Look at Life on Earth.* Oxford University Press, 1979.

Lovelock, James. *Gaia: The Practical Science of Planetary Medicine* (1991), reprinted as *Gaia: Medicine for an Ailing Planet*. London: Gaia Books, 2005.

Lovelock, James. *Homage to Gaia: The Life of an Independent Scientist*. Oxford University Press, 2000.

Lovelock, James. *The Vanishing Face of Gaia – A Final Warning*. New York: Basic Books, A Member of the Perseus Books Group, 2009.

Lozanova, Sarah. "Dutch Prepare for Climate Change With Floating Houses." *Clean Technica*. http://www.cleantechnicacom.

Mangor, Karsten. 2004: Shoreline Management Guidelines. *DHI Water and Environment*.

Margulis, Lynn. *The Symbiotic Planet*. London: Phoenix Press, 1998.

McGuffie, Kendal and Ann Henderson-Sellers. *A Climate Modeling Primer*. Chichester: Wiley, 2005.

Meadows, Donella H., Dennis L. Meadows, Jorgen Randers and William W. Behrens III. *The Limits to Growth – A Report for The Club of Rome's Project on the Predicament of Mankind*. Universe Books, 1974.

Midgely, Mary. *Science and Poetry*. London: Routledge, 2002.

Muller, Richard A. *Energy for Future Presidents: The Science Behind the Headlines*. New York: W.W. Norton & Company, 2012.

Mumford, Lewis. *The City in History: Its Origins, Its Transformations, and its Prospects.* New York: Harcourt, Brace and Co., 1961.

Mumford, Lewis. *The Culture of Cities.* Second volume of Renewal of Life Series. New York: Harcourt, Brace and Co., 1938.

Mumford, Lewis. *The Highway and the City.* New York: Harvest Book, Harcourt, Brace and World, 1963.

Mumford, Lewis. *Technics of Civilization.* First volume of Renewal of Life Series. New York: Harcourt, Brace and Co., 1934.

Murphy, Jarrett. "3 Years After Hurricane Sandy, Is New York Prepared for the Next Great Storm." *The Nation*, November 2, 2015. http://www.thenation.com.

Paulson, Henry. "How to Raise Trillions for Green Investments." *New York Times*, September 20, 2016.

Perelman, Lewis J. *Energy Innovation Fixing the Technical Fix.* Intersect Publication, 2012.

Pilkey, Orrin H., Linda Pilkey-Jarvis and Keith C. Pilkey. *Retreat from a Rising Sea – Hard Choices in an Age of Climate Change.* New York: Columbia University Press, 2016.

Poladian, Charles. "These are the Countries and Regions most at Risk from Climate Change." *Ibt Times*, December 17, 2014.

Rees, Martin. *Our Final Century.* London: William Heinemann, 2003.

Roberts, David. "No country on Earth is taking the 2 degree climate target seriously." *VOX*, October 4, 2016.

Rogers, Richard. *Cities for a Small Planet.* Faber & Faber, 1997.

Rubinstein, Dana. "Study: Seaport City idea hard, but 'feasible.'" *PoliticoNewYork*, May 22, 2014.

Schneider, Stephen H. *Global Warming.* San Francisco: Sierra Club Books, 1989.

Schumacher, E.F. *A Guide for the Perplexed.* Harper Perennial, 1977.

Schumacher, E.F. *Small is Beautiful.* Harper Perennial, 1975.

Shuman, Michael. *Going Local: Creating Self-Reliant Communities in a Global Age.* Free Press, 1998; paperback by Routledge, 2000.

Shuman, Michael. *Local Dollars, Local Sense: How to Move Your Money from Wall Street to Main Street and Achieve Real Prosperity.* Chelsea Green, 2012.

Shuman, Michael. *The Local Economy Solution: How Innovative, Self-Financing Pollinator Enterprises Can Grow Jobs and Prosperity.* Chelsea Green, 2015.

Shuman, Michael. *The Small-Mart Revolution: How Local Businesses Are Beating the Global Competition.* Berrett-Koehler, 2006.

Tainter, Joseph. *The Collapse of Complex Societie*s. Cambridge: Cambridge University Press, 1988.

"Where to Reinforce, Where to Retreat." *Regional Planning Association*, Fourth Regional Plan Roundtable, March 4, 2015.

"Why India Needs Hundreds of Nuclear Reactors." *Swarajya Magazine*, February 6, 2016.

Whyte, William Hollingsworth. *City*. Doubleday, 1988.

Wilken, Timothy. "Why Market is Obsolete." *SynEarth*, September, 2009. http://www.synearth.net.

Willard, Bob. "CO2-Why 450 ppm is Dangerous and 350 is Safe," January 7, 2014. http://www.sustainabilityadvantage.com.

Williams, Stephen. "How Molten Salt Reactors Might Spell a Nuclear Energy Revolution." *ZME Science*, January 25, 2015. http://www.zmescience.com.

Wilson, Edward O. *Consilience*. London: Little Brown and Company, 1998.

Wilson, Edward O. *The Diversity of Life*. Cambridge, MA: Harvard University Press, 1992.

Worth, Katie. "Can FEMA's Flood Insurance Program Afford Another Disaster." *PBS*, May 24, 2016. http://pbs.org.

Zolli, Andrew and Ann Marie Healey. *Resilience: Why Things Bounce Back*. New York: Free Press, Simon & Schuster, Inc., 2012.

ENDNOTES

1   Review of Elizabeth Kolbert's book, The Sixth Extinction, by Michiko Kakutani, "Cataclysm Has Arrived: Man's Inhumanity to Nature," *New York Times*, February 3, 2014.
2   Kakutani, "Cataclysm Has Arrived."
3   Viviane Richter, "The big five mass extinctions," *Cosmos*, accessed November 15, 2016, http://www.cosmosmagazine.com.
4   Brian Clark Howard, "What Antarctica's Incredible 'Growing' Icepack Really Means," *National Geographic*, November 3, 2015.
5   Cook et al., "Consensus on Consensus," *Skeptical Science*, 2016, accessed January 10, 2017, http://www.scepticalscience.com.
6   Bob Berwyn, "Far From Turning a Corner, Global CO2 Emissions Still Accelerating," *Inside Climate News*, May 19, 2016.
7   Berwyn, "Far From Turning a Corner."
8   Berwyn, "Far From Turning a Corner."
9   Citing EPA, Berwyn, "Far From Turning a Corner."
10 John Upton, "Sinking Atlantic Coastline Meets Rapidly Rising Seas," April 14, 2016, *Climate Central*, http://www.climatecentral.org.
11 Citing research by the Deltares Research Institute in Utrecht, Sarah Griffith, "Coastal Megacities Sinking Faster Than Sea Level is Rising: New Study," *Daily Mail*, January 1, 2014, accessed January 10, 2017, http://www.thegwpf.com.
12 Steven Hawkins, *BBC Radio 4 - U.K.*, broadcasts on January 26 and February 2, 2016, accessed November 15, 2016, http://www.youtube.com/watch?v=G6SKUOoTo4g/.
13 Elizabeth Howell, "How Long Have Humans Been On Earth," *Universe Today*, updated December 23, 2015, accessed December 26, 2015, http://www.universetoday.com.
14 The Club of Rome was a global think tank of world citizens established in 1968 at the Accademia dei Lincei in Rome, Italy, in *Wikipedia*, accessed December 20, 2016.
15 World population forecast, accessed December 23, 2016, http://www.worldometers.info.
16 Some changes made to punctuation after reviewing various

sources to preserve flow of Blake's poem, such sources include, for example, Colin Penter, "William Blake, The Price of Experience (1797), October 10, 2010, http://www.colinpenter.blogspot.com; *goodreads*, accessed on March 6, 2017, http://www.goodreads.com.

[17] On how Virgin Galactic seeks to provide space orbital flights in the future, Elizabeth Howell, "Virgin Galactic: Richard Branson's Space Tourism Company," *Space.com*, February 17, 2016, http://www.space.com.

[18] Venus Project, accessed on December 3, 2016, http://www.thevenusproject.com.

[19] Timothy Wilken, "Why Market is Obsolete," *SynEarth*, September, 2009, http://www.synearth.net.

[20] "Global C02 Concentrations Just Passed 400 Parts Per Million," *350.org*, accessed January 5, 2017, http://www.400.350.org.

[21] Lester R. Brown, *Plan B 3.0: Mobilizing to Save Civilization* (New York: W. W. Norton & Company, 2008), 213-87; Lester R. Brown, Janet Larsen, Jonathan G. Dorn and Frances C. Moore, "Time for Plan B: Cutting Carbon Emissions 80 Percent by 2020," *Earth Policy Institute*, accessed January 5, 2017, http://www.earth-policy.org.

[22] "Towards a Green Economy: Pathway to Sustainable Development and Poverty Eradication," *UNEP*, 2011, http://www.unep.org/greeneconomy.

[23] UNEP, "Towards a Green Economy."

[24] "The Three Pillars of Sustainability," *thwink.org*, accessed March 16, 2017, https://www.thwink.org.

[25] Intelligen power systems, accessed on December 3, 2016, http://www.intelligenpower.com.

[26] Carbon tax, accessed December 3, 2016, http://www.carbontax.org.

[27] A corporatocracy refers to an economic and political system controlled by corporations or corporate interests, in *Wikipedia*, accessed December 20, 2016.

[28] Natural Resilience Fund d/b/a Natural Resilience Foundation, accessed December 4, 2016, http://www.naturalresiliencefund.org.

29 IUPAC definition of plastic, in *Wikipedia*, accessed October 1, 2016.

30 IUPAC definition of plastic.

31 Jess Bidgood, "A Wrenching Decision Where Black History and Floods Intertwine," *New York Times*, December 9, 2016.

32 New York Wheel, accessed December 1, 2016, http://www.newyorkwheel.com.

33 The 2005 Multi-Hazard Mitigation Council Study, performed by the National Institute of Building Sciences under a commission by The Federal Emergency Management Agency, accessed December 1, 2016, http://www.nibs.org.

34 The NYC SIRR (New York City Special Initiative for Rebuilding and Resiliency) hosted several seminars including one on resiliency.

35 Henry Paulson, "How to Raise Trillions for Green Investments," *New York Times*, September 20, 2016.

36 As reported in various media outlets, the components of the one trillion dollar infrastructure plan is still being considered, with concepts such as an infrastructure bank, public private partnerships, a one-time tax on repatriated offshore business income, in Lauren Gardner, "Trump's $1 trillion plan hits D.C. speed bumps," *Politico*, November 20, 2016, http://www.politico.com; Edward Yardeni, "Get the Shovel Out: Trump's $1Trillion Infrastructure Stimulus Pledge," *Newmax Finance*, December 14, 2016, http://www.newsmax.com.

37 Dana Rubinstein, "Study: Seaport City idea hard, but 'feasible,'" *PoliticoNewYork*, May 22, 2014, http://www.politico.com.

38 Global Climate Adaptation Partnership, accessed December 5, 2016, http://www.climateadaptation.cc.

39 David Hasemyer, "Class-Action Lawsuit Adds to ExxonMobil's Climate Change Woes," *Inside Climate News*, November 21, 2016.

40 Hasemyer, "Class-Action Lawsuit Adds to ExxonMobil's Climate Change Woes."

41 "Exxon Mobil addressing climate change," accessed December 23, 2016, http://www.corporate.exxonmobil.com.

42 Kieran Cooke, "Exxon, Shell, Total, Statoil renew clean energy drive," *Climate News Network*, May 23, 2016, accessed January 8, 2017, http://www.climatechangenews.com.

43 Alliance for Climate Education, accessed January 22, 2017, http://www.acespace.org.

44 See generally "Economics of Biofuels," *EPA*, May 27, 2016, accessed January 22, 2017, http://www.epa.gov.

45 Hoesung Lee, Chair of Intergovernmental Panel on Climate Change. "Climate 2020: Rising to the challenge," *United Nations Association–UK*, 24-26.

46 John Schwartz, "Can Carbon Capture Technology Prosper Under Trump," *New York Times*, last updated January 2, 2017.

47 Schwartz, "Can Carbon Capture Technology Prosper Under Trump."

48 Sebastian Anthony, "Thorium nuclear reactor trial begins, could provide cleaner, safer, almost-waste-free energy," *Extreme Tech*, July 1, 2013, http://www.extremetech.com.

49 "Molten Salt Reactors," *World Nuclear Association*, updated September 30, 2016, http://www.world-nuclear.org.

50 Iain McClatchie comments to blog entitled "if Thorium (LFTR) reactors are so awesome, why hasn't anyone built one yet," updated June 2, 2014, http://www.quora.com; Staff Writer, "Why India Needs Hundreds of Nuclear Reactors," *Swarajya Magazine*, February 6, 2016, http://www.swarajyamag.com; Neil Endicot, "Thorium-Fuelled Molten Salt Reactors," *Weinberg Foundation*, http://www.the-weinberg-foundation.org.

51 Thorium molten salt reactor, in *Wikipedia*, accessed December 7, 2016, http://www.thmsr.nl.

52 Higher levels of actinides remain in conventional nuclear reactors as compared to MSRs because the ceramic rods crack before most of the actinides split, in Stephen Williams, "How Molten Salt Reactors Might Spell a Nuclear Energy Revolution," *ZME Science*, January 25, 2015, http://www.zmescience.com.

53 Williams, "How Molten Salt Reactors Might Spell a Nuclear Energy Revolution."

54 Williams, "How Molten Salt Reactors Might Spell a Nuclear Energy Revolution."

55 "Geothermal Heating and Cooling Technologies," *EPA*, December 19, 2016, accessed on January 22, 2017, http://www.epa.gov.

56 Dutch ATES, accessed December 23, 2016, http://www.dutch-ates.com.

57 Citing the research work of PhD candidate Zhubiao Ni in "Faster groundwater remediation with thermal storage," *Wageningen University Press Release*, December 8, 2015.

58 "Faster groundwater remediation with thermal storage."

59 James Lovelock, *The Vanishing Face of Gaia – A Final Warning* (Basic Books, A Member of the Perseus Books Group, 2009), 68.

60 Practical Action, accessed December 3, 2016, http://www.practicalaction.org.

61 E. F. Schumacher, *Small is Beautiful – Economics as if People Mattered* (Harper Perennial, 1971), 13-14.

62 Practical Action.

63 Practical Action.

64 Practical Action.

65 The Editorial Board, "The Climate Refugees of the Arctic," *New York Times*, December 20, 2016; Erica Goode, "Polar Bears' Path to Decline Runs Through Alaskan Village," *New York Times*, December 18, 2016.

66 Christine Dell'Amore, "7 Species Hit Hard by Climate Change— Including One That's Already Extinct," *National Geographic*, April 2, 2014.

67 "Pollination," Michigan State University Native Plants and Ecosystem Service, accessed December 27, 2016, http://www.nativeplants.msu.edu.

68 Buckminster Fuller cited by Patricia Ravasio, "Calling All Spaceship Earth Crew," accessed December 23, 2016, http://www.buckyworld.me.

69 Netherlands, in *Wikipedia*, accessed December 15, 2016.

70 Netherlands, *Wikipedia*.

71 Bangladesh in *Wikipedia*, accessed December 15, 2016.

72 "Dhaka, Bangladesh: Fastest Growing City in the World," *Global Post CBS News*, September 19, 2010, accessed January 8, 2017, http://www.cbsnews.com.

73   Katie Worth, "Can FEMA's Flood Insurance Program Afford Another Disaster," *PBS*, May 24, 2016, http://www.pbs.org.
74   Worth, "Can FEMA's Flood Insurance Program Afford Another Disaster."
75   Worth, "Can FEMA's Flood Insurance Program Afford Another Disaster."
76   "Why 2 degrees Celsius is climate change's magic number," *PBS Newshour*, December 2, 2015, http://www.pbs.com.
77   Citing William Brangham in PBS Newshour, "Why 2 degrees Celsius is climate change's magic number."
78   David Roberts, "No country on Earth is taking the 2 degree climate target seriously," *VOX*, October 4, 2016, http://www.vox.com.
79   Citing International Energy Agency, in Roberts, "No country on Earth is taking the 2 degree climate target seriously."
80   Citing projections in report by Oil Change International as well as David Roberts and Glen Peters, in Roberts, "No country on Earth is taking the 2 degree climate target seriously."
81   Brown, Larsen, Dorn and Moore, "Time for Plan B"; citing "OECD Environmental Outlook to 2050: Key Findings on Climate Change," in Bob Willard, "CO2-Why 450 ppm is Dangerous and 350 is Safe," January 7, 2014.
82   Charles Poladian, "These are the Countries and Regions most at Risk from Climate Change," *Ibt Times*, December 17, 2014, http://www.ibtimes.com.
83   Ana Swanson, "The countries most vulnerable to climate change," *Washington Post*, February 3, 2016, http://www.washingtonpost.com.
84   Swanson, "The countries most vulnerable to climate change."
85   Michele Berger, "The weather.com Climate Disruption Index - 25 U.S. Cities Most Affected by Climate Change," http://www.stories.weather.com.
86   Berger, "The weather.com Climate Disruption Index."
87   "Is Sea Level Rising," NOAA's National Ocean Service, accessed January 26, 2017, http://www.oceanservice.noaa.gov.
88   Timothy M. Lenton, "Arctic Climate Tipping Points," January 22, 2012, http://www.ncbi.nlmnih.gov.

89   We support the use of electric cars understanding that the technology on lithium batteries needs to be improved so they are eco-friendly.

90   Sarah Lozanova, "Dutch Prepare for Climate Change With Floating Houses," *Clean Technica*, accessed December 27, 2016, http://www.cleantechnicacom.

91   Nicholas Kristof, "As Donald Trump Denies Climate Change, These Kids Die of It," *New York Times*, updated January 6, 2017.

92   Kristof, "As Donald Trump Denies Climate Change."

93   Kristof, "As Donald Trump Denies Climate Change."

94   Peter S. Goodman, "Free Cash in Finland. Must Be Jobless," *New York Times*, December 17, 2016.

95   New Orleans, in *Wikipedia*, accessed December 1, 2016.

96   Jarrett Murphy, "3 Years After Hurricane Sandy, Is New York Prepared for the Next Great Storm," November 2, 2015, http://www.thenation.com.

97   John Burnett, "Billions Spent on Flood Barriers, but New Orleans still a 'Fishbowl,'" August 28, 2015, http://www.NPR.org.

98   Burnett, "Billions Spent on Flood Barriers."

99   Citing Mike Park, the Corps' chief of operations in New Orleans, in Burnett, "Billions Spent on Flood Barriers."

100 Thomas Kaplan, "Cuomo Seeking Home Buyouts in Flood Zone," *New York Times*, February 3, 2013.

101 Vishaan Chakrabarti, *A Country of Cities: A Manifesto for an Urban America* (Metropolis Books, 2013).

102 A figure provided by Al Gore during a presentation for Millennials at the Marriott Marquis in New York City around October 2014.

103 Kristen King, "Press Release: Assets Pledged To Fossil Fuel Divestment Surpass $5 Trillion Says New Report," *DivestInvest*, in John Schwartz, "Investment Funds Worth Trillions Are Dropping Fossil Fuel Stocks," *New York Times*, December 12, 2016.

104 Schwartz, "Investment Funds Worth Trillions Are Dropping Fossil Fuel Stocks."

105 "The Climate Accountability Scorecard: Ranking Major Fossil Fuel Companies on Climate Deception, Disclosure, and Action

(2016)," *Union of Concerned Scientists*, accessed January 5, 2017, http://www.uscusa.org.

106 "The Climate Accountability Scorecard."

107 "The Climate Accountability Scorecard."

108 Paul Sullivan, "Trump May Not Like Alternative Energy, but Investors Should," *New York Times*, January 6, 2017.

109 Sullivan, "Trump May Not Like Alternative Energy, but Investors Should."

110 For example, in California "household water use is much lower in multifamily buildings than in single-family homes. Roughly half of all water use in the residential sector in California is outdoor use, primarily landscape irrigation. Apartment dwellers, with far less yard space per household, have lower levels of household water use than those living in single-family homes." Ed Osann, "Flawed Analysis Muddies the Water on Water Affordability," *National Resource Defense Council*, June 20, 2016, accessed January 10, 2017, http://www.nrdc.org.

111 Quoting Barb Cooper, 2015 President of the Austin Board of Realtors in "September 2015 statistics," *Austin Board of Realtors*, October 22, 2015, http://www.advantage.com.

112 "Texas Sales and Use Tax Revenue for Transportation Amendment, Proposition 7 (2015)," accessed November 20, 2016, http://www.ballotpedia.org.

113 The seven U.S. states relying on the Colorado River are: California, Nevada, Arizona, Texas, Colorado, Utah and New Mexico; and the two Mexican states that receive about 3% of the River's waters are Baja California and Sonora.

114 "Coals and jobs in the United States," Center for Media and Democracy, *Sourcewatch*, accessed, January 10, 2017, http://www.sourcewatch.org; Bureau of Labor Statistics (April 2016).

115 "Coals and jobs in the United States," *Sourcewatch*.

116 "Coals and jobs in the United States," *Sourcewatch*.

117 "Coals and jobs in the United States," *Sourcewatch*.

118 "Coals and jobs in the United States," *Sourcewatch*.

119 Joe Smyth, "Three coal companies are trying to keep secret how much federal coal they mine," *Climate Investigations Center*, Octo-

ber 12, 2016, accessed January 12, 2017,
http://www.climateinvestigations.org.

120 "Coal: A Long History of Subsidies," *Taxpayers for Common Sense*,
accessed January 10, 2017, http://www.taxpayer.net.

121 Of the 1 million residents in Cartagena, 600,000 are poor and
"tens of thousands" are destitute, Juan Forero, "In Colombia
newfound wealth masks poverty," *Washington Post*, February 1,
2009, http://www.archive.boston.com.

122 Under the Homesteading Act of 1862, "adult citizens who paid a
registration fee, agreed to live on the land continuously for five
years," from a pool of public land grants, and later "proved up"
their claim were granted title to the land. The underlying policy,
among other factors, was to settle and make these lands productive. These days homesteading is about self-sufficiency – "using
less energy, eating wholesome local food," and being part of the
community for a better "quality of life for the family, community
and environment." Heidi Hunt, Homesteading and Livestock,"
Mother Earth News, July 13, 2007,
http://www.motherearthnews.com.

123 Map entitled Figure 1. Growing Risks to Homes from Sea Level
Rise and Storms, based on data from Strauss et al. 2012, "Over-
whelming Risk: Rethinking Flood Insurance in a World of Rising
Seas," *Union of Concerned Scientists*, 4, accessed January 6, 2017,
http://www.ucsusa.org.

124 Song entitled "A Change is Gonna Come" from *Ain't that Good
News*, Sam Cooke (RCA Victor, 1964).

125 Strauss, B. H., Kulp, S. and Levermann, A. 2015, "Mapping
Choices: Carbon, Climate, and Rising Seas, Our Global Legacy,"
Climate Central Research Report, 1-38,
http://www.sealevel.climatecentral.org.

126 Maps courtesy of Climate Central; accessed December 26, 2016,
http://www.sealevel.climatecentral.org.

127 "New York and The Surging Sea: A Vulnerability Assessment
With Projections For Sea Level Rise and Coastal Flood Risk"
Climate Central, updated April 2014, Appendix D,
http://cwww.climatecentral.org.

[128] In the table named "Climate Central Top Zip Codes at Risk below 9 Ft," we named our second column to be the area, population, number of housing units and property value affected or "below 9' ft of water" as opposed to the second column heading of their Appendix D table saying "State Total Below 6' ft" of water. We made this change to correspond with the name of their table, Appendix D: Tables of Exposure at 9 feet Mean High Higher Water, and the headers of their other columns which all refer to 9 ft. This change also is consistent with our third column that is also drawn from their table entitled "New York and The Surging Sea."

[129] Maps courtesy of Climate Central; accessed December 26, 2016, http://www.sealevel.climatecentral.org.

[130] "Sea level rise and coastal flood risk: Summary for New Orleans, LA," *Climate Central*, created July 21, 2016, http://ssrf.climatecentral.org.s3-website-us-east1.amazonaws.com/Buffer2/states/LA/downloads/pdf_reports/Town/LA_New_Orleansreport.pdf.

[131] "Sea level rise and coastal flood risk: Summary for Los Angeles County, CA," Climate Central, created July 21, 2016, http://ssrf.climatecentral.org.s3-website-us-east-1.amazonaws.com/Buffer2/states/CA/downloads/pdf_reports/County/CA_Los_Angeles_County-report.pdf.

[132] Maps courtesy of Climate Central; accessed December 26, 2016, http://www.sealevel.climatecentral.org.

[133] Lovelock, *The Vanishing Face of Gaia*.

[134] Lovelock, *The Vanishing Face of Gaia*.

[135] Lovelock, *The Vanishing Face of Gaia*.

[136] Built environment, in *Wikipedia* accessed November 29, 2016.

[137] Cap and trade, accessed November 1, 2016, http://www.edf.org.

[138] OECD Glossary of Statistical Terms.

[139] Carbon tax, accessed December 1, 2016, http://www.carbontax.org.

[140] COP21, accessed December 1, 2016, http://www.cop21.gouv.fr.

[141] Business resilience, accessed December 3, 2016, http://www.techtarget.com.

142 Jeffrey Sachs, *The Price of Civilization: Reawakening American Virtue and Prosperity* (Random House, October 4, 2011 in the US and by Bodley Head in UK, Oct 6, 2011).

143 Corporatocracy, in *Wikipedia*, accessed December 15, 2016.

144 Deforestation, accessed October 12, 2016, http://www.dictionary.com.

145 David W. Dunlap, "A Guide to Flood-Resistant Building Terms," *New York Times*, January 25, 2017.

146 Lovelock, *The Vanishing Face of Gaia*.

147 Green economy, in *Wikipedia*, accessed November 29, 2016.

148 Lovelock, *The Vanishing Face of Gaia*.

149 Dunlap, "A Guide to Flood-Resistant Building Terms."

150 Dunlap, "A Guide to Flood-Resistant Building Terms."

151 "Ice Caps, Ice Sheets, and Ice Shelves: What's the Difference," *NASA*, Exploring the Environment, accessed January 10, 2017, http://www.ete.cet.edu.

152 "The Canary in the Gold Mine."

153 "Ice Caps, Ice Sheets, and Ice Shelves."

154 Investment subsidies, in *Investopedia*, accessed December 3, 2016.

155 Investment tax credits, accessed December 3, 2016, http://www.dictionary.com.

156 Leed Certification, accessed December 3, 2016, http://techtarget.com.

157 Lovelock, *The Vanishing Face of Gaia*.

158 Managed retreat, in *Wikipedia*, accessed November 29, 2016.

159 Methane, accessed November 29, 2016, http://www.dictionary.com.

160 Berwyn, "Far From Turning a Corner."

161 Multiplier effect in *The American Heritage ® New Dictionary of Cultural Literacy*, Third Edition (Houghton Mifflin Company, 2005).

162 "Urban Waterfront Adaptive Strategies," *NYC Planning, Department of City Planning City of New York*, June 2013, 86.

163 Uranium, accessed November 29, 2016, http://www.eia.gov/energyexplained.

164 "Global CO2 Concentrations Just Passed 400 Parts Per Million."

165 Lovelock, *The Vanishing Face of Gaia*.

166 Renewable energy, accessed December 2, 2016,
http://www.dictionary.com.
167 Resilience, in *Wikipedia*, accessed November 29, 2016.
168 "Where to Reinforce, Where to Retreat," *Regional Planning Association*, Fourth Regional Plan Roundtable, March 4, 2015.
169 Karsten Mangor, 2004: Shoreline Management Guidelines. *DHI Water and Environment.*
170 Dunlap, "A Guide to Flood-Resistant Building Terms."
171 Stranded asset, in *Investor Dictionary*, accessed November 29, 2016.
172 Upton, "Sinking Atlantic Coastline Meets Rapidly Rising Seas."
173 Citing conclusions and results from new loss model developed by Swiss Re and Swiss Federal Institute of Technology, "Climate change contributing to surge in subsidence damage," *The Actuary*, The Institute and Faculty of Actuaries, accessed January 10, 2017, http://www.theactuary.com.
174 Sunk costs, in *Investor Dictionary*, accessed November 29, 2016.
175 Sustainability, accessed December 2, 2016,
http://www.dictionary.com.
176 Dunlap, "A Guide to Flood-Resistant Building Terms."
177 Fragile states index, accessed December 21, 2016,
http://www.fst.fundforpeace.org.
178 Timothy M. Lenton, "Arctic Climate Tipping Points," January 22, 2012, http://www.ncbi.nlmnih.gov.
179 Quoting the text from "Historic Paris Agreement on Climate Change," *UNFCC Newsroom*, December 12, 2005,
http://www.newsroom.unfccc.int.
180 Red Oaks Trading, Ltd., Reno, NV 89509.
181 Abraham Maslow, accessed November 4, 2016,
http://www.simplypsychology.org

INDEX